LITIGATION LIBRARY

DISCLOSURE

First Supplement
Fifth Edition

Litigation Library

DISCLOSURE

FIRST SUPPLEMENT
FIFTH EDITION

by

Paul Matthews, B.C.L. (Oxon), LL.D. (Lond.)
Master, High Court, Chancery Division
A Recorder (Civil)
Visiting Professor, King's College, London
formerly H.M. Coroner for the City of London

and

Hodge M. Malek QC, B.C.L., M.A. (Oxon.)
One of Her Majesty's Counsel,
A Bencher of Gray's Inn
A Recorder of the Crown Court
Chairman of the Competition Appeal Tribunal

SWEET & MAXWELL   THOMSON REUTERS

Published in 2019 by Thomson Reuters,
trading as Sweet & Maxwell. Thomson Reuters is registered in
England & Wales, Company No.1679046. Registered Office and address for service:
5 Canada Square, Canary Wharf, London, E14 5AQ.
For further information on our products and services, visit
http://www.sweetandmaxwell.co.uk.

Typeset by Wright & Round Ltd, Gloucestershire
Printed and bound in Great Britain by CPI Group (UK) Ltd, Croydon, CR0 4YY.

No natural forests were destroyed to make this product;
only farmed timber was used and replanted.

A CIP catalogue record for this book is available from the British Library.

ISBN 978-0-414-07011-0

Thomson Reuters and the Thomson Reuters Logo are trademarks of
Thomson Reuters.
Sweet & Maxwell is a registered trademark of Thomson Reuters.
Crown copyright material is reproduced with the permission
of the Controller of HMSO and the Queen's Printer for Scotland.

HOW TO USE THIS SUPPLEMENT

This is the First Supplement to *Disclosure* (being the fifth edition of *Discovery*), and has been compiled according to the structure of the main volume.

At the beginning of each chapter of this Supplement is a mini table of contents from the main volume. Where a heading in this table of contents has been marked by an asterisk, this indicates that there is relevant information in the Supplement to which the reader should refer.

Within each chapter, updating information is referenced to the relevant paragraph in the main volume.

The Table of Cases refers to all the cases cited in this Supplement.

CONTENTS

Chapter 5
What Must be Disclosed

Chapter 6
Means of Disclosure

Chapter 10
Production by Non-Parties

Chapter 11
Objections to Inspection (1): Introductioin and Legal Professional Privilege

Chapter 12
Objections to Inspection (2): Public Interest Immunity

Chapter 14
Objections to Inspection (4): "Without Prejudice" Privilege

TABLE OF CASES

TABLE OF STATUTES IN SUPPLEMENT

TABLE OF STATUTORY INSTRUMENTS IN SUPPLEMENT

TABLE OF CIVIL PROCEDURE RULES IN SUPPLEMENT

CHAPTER 1

Introduction

CHAPTER 1

Introduction

F. REFORM AND THE CIVIL PROCEDURE RULES 1998

Add new paragraphs at end:

In May 2016 the Chancellor of the High Court, Sir Terence Etherton, **1.36** established the Disclosure Working Group chaired by Dame Elizabeth Gloster in response to concerns expressed by court users and the profession regarding the perceived excessive costs, scale and complexity of disclosure. Essentially, the Disclosure Working Group found that these concerns were justified particularly in substantial cases commonly before Business and Property Courts in England and Wales.

The Working Group proposed a pilot scheme under a Practice Direction, with a Disclosure Review Document ("DRD") in place of the existing Electronic Disclosure Questionnaire. The Practice Direction 51U Disclosure pilot for the Business and Property Courts was approved by the Civil Procedure Rule Committee in June 2018 and came into effect on 1 January 2019. The Pilot Scheme and Practice Direction apply (with limited exceptions) to existing and new proceedings across the Business and Property Courts in the Rolls Building and in the centres of Bristol, Birmingham, Cardiff, Leeds, Liverpool and Manchester for a two-year period.

It is envisaged that in the light of the results of the Pilot Scheme, CPR Pt.31 will be replaced or substantially revised.

The Disclosure Working Group press announcement on 31 July 2018 summarised the key changes introduced by the Disclosure Pilot as follows:

(1) The principles upon which disclosure is based are now clearly stated in the practice direction.
(2) What has been termed "standard disclosure" has been removed in its current form; its replacement (Model D) should not be ordered in every case and will not be regarded as the default form of disclosure.
(3) The duties of the parties, and of their lawyers, in relation to disclosure are expressly set out. These include a duty to cooperate so as

to promote the reliable, efficient and cost-effective conduct of disclosure. They also include a duty to disclose known adverse documents in all cases, irrespective of whether an order to do so is made.

(4) The duty to disclose known documents that are adverse to a party's case has been strengthened and is now wider than the obligation under Pt.31.

(5) Unless dispensed with by agreement or order (and subject to several other exceptions), "Initial Disclosure" will be given with statements of case of key documents which are relied on by the disclosing party and are necessary for other parties to understand the case they have to meet. A search should not be required for Initial Disclosure, although one may be undertaken. Initial Disclosure is not intended to be an onerous process (generally it should comprise no more than 200 documents or 1,000 pages) and there are several exceptions where it can be dispensed with entirely. For some cases, Initial Disclosure may obviate the need for any further disclosure (in whole or in part).

(6) After closure of statements of case, and before the case management conference, the parties should be required to meet, discuss and complete a joint Disclosure Review Document to:

(a) List the Issues for Disclosure in the case (those key issues in dispute which the court will need to determine with some reference to contemporaneous documents);

(b) Exchange proposals for "Extended Disclosure" (including which Disclosure Models should apply for which issue(s)); and

(c) Share information about how documents are stored and how they might (if required) be searched and reviewed (including with the assistance of technology).

(7) The DRD provides a mandatory framework for parties and their advisers to cooperate and engage prior to the first case management conference with a view to agreeing a proportionate and efficient approach to disclosure.

(8) At the case management conference, the court should consider which of five "Extended Disclosure" models (Models A to E) is to apply to which issue (or to all issues). The models range from an order for disclosure of known adverse documents only on particular Issues for Disclosure, through to the widest form of disclosure, requiring the production of documents which may lead to a train of enquiry.

(9) The court should be proactive in directing which is the appropriate Disclosure Model and should not accept without question the Disclosure Model proposed by the parties.

(10) With a view to encouraging increased and more focused case management, the practice direction identifies a range of orders which the court may make to reduce the burden and cost of disclosure.

(11) Further, the parties can apply for a Disclosure Guidance Hearing to seek informal guidance from the court before or after a case management conference. These hearings should be used as an informal means of overcoming an impasse reached by the parties.

(12) When considering what orders to make on disclosure, the well-recognised test of reasonableness and proportionality is now applied by reference to defined criteria at para.6.4 of the draft Practice Direction, which are relevant to disclosure. This test builds upon the overriding objective.

(13) In order to inform the court's decision on Extended Disclosure, the parties are under an express Disclosure Duty to cooperate and engage before the case management conference so that the court can be informed: (a) of any joint view as to the Disclosure Model that should apply; and (b) of the estimated work and cost of using any Disclosure Model that is proposed by one or more of the parties.

(14) Where cost budgeting applies, Form H Cost Budgets in relation to disclosure will still need to be completed in the usual way unless it is not practical to do so, in which case completion of the disclosure section in Form H will be postponed until after the case management conference.

(15) In addition, parties will be required to give estimates of the likely costs of disclosure when filing the completed DRD in order that the question of proportionality may be considered at the CMC before an order for disclosure is made.

(16) Finally, the practice direction sets out the range of orders and sanctions for noncompliance with the requirements of the new scheme and, in particular, the new duties on the parties and their advisers.

CHAPTER 2

Time of Disclosure

CHAPTER 2

Time of Disclosure

B. AT THE TIME PROCEEDINGS ARE COMMENCED

(a) Orders ancillary to injunctions

At the end of fn.60 add:

[60] In *JSC BTA Bank v Ablyazov and Khrapunov* [2018] EWHC 1368 (Comm) a defendant   **2.13**
who was subject to a worldwide freezing order was ordered to provide disclosure regarding the
way in which his legal expenses were being funded. In such a case the claimant must establish
that there are adequate grounds for making the order. As noted in *JSC Mezhprom Bank v
Pugachev* [2017] EWHC 1847 (Ch) at [71], the court may make an order where there is a
properly arguable case that the funding is or may be from frozen funds. The threshold test is
whether the evidence establishes a risk that is real, and not fanciful, breach of the freezing
order. Once this is met, the strength (or otherwise) of the evidence is then a factor which needs
to be weighed with other considerations for and against an order (*Ablyazov* at [16]).

At the end of fn.62 add:

[62] In *Khrapunov v JSC BTA Bank* [2018] EWCA Civ 819, CA an order was made against a   **2.13**
defendant for his cross-examination in respect of assets he owned or controlled. This was with
a view to ensuring the effectiveness of a worldwide freezing order. It was held that he should
give such evidence in court in London, rather than by video-link from Switzerland as the latter
would be less effective.

D. DISCLOSURE AFTER JUDGMENT HAS BEEN GIVEN

Oral examination

Add new paragraphs at end:

In *Vik v Deutsche Bank* [2018] EWCA Civ 2011 a former director and   **2.48**
shareholder of the judgment debtor company residing outside the jurisdiction, was served within the jurisdiction with an order under CPR r.71.2
requiring him to provide documents and attend the court for cross-examination about the judgment debtors' means. Upon his failure to comply with
the order, various issues as to the proper procedure and jurisdiction to make
and serve a committal application against him at a time he was not residing

within the jurisdiction. The Court of Appeal laid down the following principles:

(1) A party seeking to hold a person in contempt for failure to comply with a CPR r.71.2 order is not confined to making it under CPR r.71.8 (which may lack extraterritorial reach), may apply under CPR r.81.4 (which has extraterritorial reach).

(2) Applications under CPR r.71.8 are more suitable for straightforward cases of breach, as opposed to more complex applications under CPR r.81.4.

(3) As a committal application is incidental to a CPR 71 order, there is no requirement to seek permission to serve it on a person residing outside of the jurisdiction.

(4) There was considerable force in Teare J's view that there is no specific jurisdictional gateway in PD6B permitting service out of the jurisdiction of an application to commit an officer of a company for contempt of an order made under CPR Part 81 or 71, notwithstanding that the fact that the officer is out of the jurisdiction is no bar to the making of such an application.

CHAPTER 3

Norwich Pharmacal and other Pre-Action Disclosure

CHAPTER 3

Norwich Pharmacal and other Pre-Action Disclosure

A. NORWICH PHARMACAL ORDERS

Add new paragraph at end:

For a discussion of the basis of the duty to assist in the *Norwich Pharmacal*   **3.03**
jurisdiction on a person who has been mixed up in the tortious acts of
others, see *Singularis Holdings Ltd v PriceWaterhouseCoopers* [2015] AC
1675 at [22] and *Cartier International AG v British Sky Broadcasting Ltd*
[2018] UKSC 28, [2018] 1 W.L.R. 3259 at [10-11] (Lord Sumption). The
duty to assist is not a legal duty in the ordinary sense of the term. See also
Lederer v Allsop LLP [2018] EWHC 1425 (Ch) (specific disclosure ordered
of identity of lenders under loan agreement arranged by P2P agency).

Requirements

Add new paragraph at end:

The principles for a *Norwich Pharmacal* order set out in *Ramilos Trading*   **3.04**
Ltd v Buyanovsky [2016] EWHC 3175 at [11], were applied in *Miles Smith
Broking Ltd v Barclays* [2017] EWHC 3338 (Ch).

Add new paragraph at end:

The first sentence of this paragraph was cited with approval in *Miles Smith*   **3.05**
Broking Ltd v Barclays Bank Plc [2017] EWHC 3338 (Ch) at [10].

At the end of fn.28 add:

[28] *Ho v Lloyds Bank plc*, 31 January 2018 unreported QBD.   **3.05**

Add new paragraph at end:

In *Ramilos Trading Ltd v Buyanovsky* [2016] EWHC 3175 (Comm) at [33],   **3.06**
Flaux J reviewed the authorities and held that there must be a good arguable
case that a wrong has been committed.

Add new paragraph at end:

3.08 In *Ramilos Trading Ltd v Buyanovsky* [2016] EWHC 3175 (Comm) at [111], Flaux J reviewed the authorities and concluded that even if the jurisdiction may be used to obtain disclosure of limited information for use in overseas proceedings, the jurisdiction may not be used to obtain evidence for use of overseas proceedings. This is because of the statutory regime for gathering of such evidence in the Evidence (Proceedings in Other Jurisdictions) Act 1975.

Update the citation at fn.53 as follows:

3.08   [53] *AB Bank Ltd v Abu Dhabi Commercial Bank PJSC* [2016] EWHC 2082 (Comm); [2017] 1 W.L.R. 810.

Add new paragraph at end:

3.09 In *Ramilos Trading v Buyanovsky* [2016] EWHC 3175 (Comm) at [62], Flaux J stressed that the *Norwich Pharmacal* jurisdiction remained an exceptional jurisdiction with a narrow scope. The court will not permit the jurisdiction to be used for wide-ranging disclosure or the gathering of evidence, as opposed to focused disclosure of necessary information.

Add new paragraph at end:

3.16 See also *Benhurst Finance Ltd v Colliac*, 29 June 2018 unreported QBD (HHJ Nicholas Cooke QC) (order made where no more suitable route to relief was available).

Bankers Trust

Add new paragraph at end:

3.20 Usually a *Bankers Trust* claim is not opposed by the respondent bank. In such a case, the matter can be listed before a Master for a disposal hearing: *Miles Smith Broking Ltd v Barclays Bank Plc* [2017] EWHC 3338 (Ch) at [2].

Update the citation at fn.97 as follows:

3.20   [97] *A Co. v B Co.* [2002] HKCFI 1080.

Costs

Add new paragraph at end:

3.31 The ordinary rule, absent exceptional circumstances, is that the intermediary is entitled to the costs of compliance: *Cartier International AG v Sky Broadcasting Ltd* [2018] UKSC 28, [2018] 1 W.L.R. 3259 at [12]. A similar practice applies to the expenses incurred by banks in complying with orders to disclose information for the purposes of enabling a party to trace the proceedings of fraud (at [13]). The ordinary principle, in relation to a website blocking order, is that unless there are good reasons for a different order an innocent intermediary (in that case UK internet service providers) is entitled to be indemnified by the rightholder (who claimed that their trademarks were being infringed) against the costs of complying with the order (at [31]). As regards the costs of the litigation, the intermediaries are normally awarded the costs of the action. In that case it was held that the judge had been entitled to award costs against the ISPs because they had made the litigation a test case for the jurisdiction to make the order at all, and had strenuously resisted the application (at [38]).

At the end of fn.156 add:

[156] In *Pricewaterhouse Coopers v SAAD Investments Co Ltd (No 2)* [2017] 1 W.L.R. 953, the Privy Council held that where auditors of a company in liquidation did preparatory work for complying with a *Norwich Pharmacal* order later made, but subsequently set aside on appeal, the auditors could not recover those costs from the liquidators, not having sought to protect their position by *e.g.* seeking an undertaking from the liquidators beforehand.

B. PRE-ACTION DISCLOSURE: CPR RULE 31.16

Procedure

Add new paragraph at end:

The issue as to whether the court has jurisdiction to grant permission to **3.44** serve an application for pre-action disclosure out of the jurisdiction is a contentious one. In *ED&F Man Capital Markets LLP v Obex Securities LLC* [2017] EWHC 2965 (Ch), [2018] 1 W.L.R. 1708, Catherine Newman QC (sitting as a deputy High Court judge) held that there is. Under CPR r.6.36 the court has power to permit a claimant to serve a "claim form" out of the jurisdiction; she held that this jurisdiction extends to an application before action (at [13]). Paragraph 3.11(a) of CPR PD 6B provides a jurisdictional gateway where a claim is made "under an enactment which allows proceedings to be brought and those proceedings are not covered by any of the other grounds referred to in this paragraph". She held that s.33 of the Senior Courts Act 1981 falls within this gateway as in her view an application under s.33 and CPR r.31.16 for pre-action disclosure are a form of proceedings (at [23]).

C. CORPORATE INSOLVENCY

Procedure

Add new paragraph:

Under the Insolvency Rules 2016, r.14.6 an office holder of a company in **3.52A** liquidation must allow inspection of proofs of debts by a member or contributory. However, in order to obtain a court order for disclosure, the contributory not only has to demonstrate it has standing to apply for the relief, but it has a legitimate interest in that relief: *Burden Group Holdings Ltd v Hunt* [2018] EWHC 463 (Ch), [2018] B.C.C. 404.

D. APPLICATION TO INSPECT COURT FILE

(b) Inspection where permission required

Add new paragraphs at end:

3.54 In *Ashley v Blue* [2017] EWHC 1553 (Comm) a newspaper applied under CPR r.5.4C(2) for permission to obtain from the records of the court copies of two witness statements prepared for a pending trial which had been referred to at an interlocutory hearing. Leggatt J held that the fact that the court may no longer have copies of a document lodged with the court (e.g. if returned after a hearing) will not prevent the court from ensuring that a non-party can obtain a copy, if the open justice principle requires this. The court could order one of the parties to file the document again or to provide a copy directly to a non-party. He also found that there is nothing in the CPR which precludes the court from making an order under its common law powers to enable a non-party to obtain a copy of a document which has been served in the litigation, even if the document has not been filed by a party (at [10]). There are good reasons why the court should not generally make witness statements prepared for use at a trial publicly available before the witnesses give evidence (at [12]). The judge refused the application for access to copies of those statements but did allow access to statements prepared, filed and deployed at an interlocutory hearing which had taken place.

Under CPR r.5.4C(2) a non-party may, if the court gives permission, obtain from the records of the court a copy of a document filed by a party, or communications between the court and a party or another person. In *Cape Intermediate Holdings Ltd v Dring (Asbestos Victims Support Group)* [2018] EWCA Civ 1795, it was held that "records of the court" are essentially documents kept by the court officer as a record of the proceedings. The principal documents which are likely to fall under that description are set out in CPR 5A PD4, para.4.2A together with "communications between the court and a party or another person" as CPR r.5.4C(2) makes clear. In some cases there will be documents held by the court office additional to those in CPR 5A PD4, para.4.2A but they will only be "records of the court" if they are analogous in nature. In particular, records of the court include:

1. Lists of documents, but not the documents listed as well.

2. Witness statements and exhibits filed in relation to an application notice or Part 8 proceedings, but not usually witness statements or expert reports exchanged by the parties in relation to a trial.
3. The receipt document for the trial bundles, but not the bundles themselves. The principle of open justice does not require non-parties to have access to trial bundles.

Neither are skeleton arguments, opening or closing notes or submissions, or trial transcripts records of the court.

The court has an inherent jurisdiction to provide certain materials to non-parties, in particular, copies of skeleton arguments/written submissions used in lieu of oral argument. This does not extend to allowing non-parties access to trial documents generally, even if they have been referred to in a skeleton argument, witness statement, expert's report or in court (at [88]). The position was summarised as follows (at [112]):

(1) There is no inherent jurisdiction to allow non-parties inspection of:

(a) trial bundles;
(b) documents which have been referred to in witness statements, experts' reports or in open court simply on the basis that they have been referred to.

(2) There is inherent jurisdiction to allow non-parties inspection of:

(i) Witness statements of witnesses, including experts, whose evidence stands as evidence in chief and which would have been available for inspection during the course of the trial under CPR 32.13.
(ii) Documents in relation to which confidentiality has been lost under CPR 31.22 and which are read out in open court; which the judge is invited to read in open court; which the judge is specifically invited to read outside court, or which it is clear or stated that the judge has read.
(iii) Skeleton arguments/written submissions or similar advocate's documents read by the court provided that there is an effective public hearing in which the documents are deployed.
(iv) Any specific document or documents which it is necessary for a non-party to inspect in order to meet the principle of open justice.

As to the principles to be applied when the court is considering whether and how to exercise its discretion to grant permission for copies to be obtained by a non-party of the records of the court under 5.4C(2), the court has to balance the non-party's reasons for seeking copies of the documents against the party to the proceedings' private interest in preserving their confidentiality. Relevant factors are likely to include:

17

1. The extent to which the open justice principle is engaged.
2. Whether the documents are sought in the interests of open justice.
3. Whether there is a legitimate interest in seeking copies of the documents and, if so, whether that is a public or private interest.
4. The reasons for seeking to preserve confidentiality.
5. The harm, if any, which may be caused by access to the documents to the legitimate interests of other parties (at [127]).

CHAPTER 4

Persons Who Must Give Disclosure

CHAPTER 4

Persons Who Must Give Disclosure

A. GENERAL POSITION OF SUBSTANTIVE PARTIES TO PROCEEDINGS

(6) Judicial review

Add new paragraph at end:

In *R (Slade) v Attorney General* [2018] EWHC 1451 (Admin) an applica- 4.07
tion for specific disclosure was refused in judicial review proceedings of the
defendant's refusal to investigate the CPS's decision to prosecute the claimants for offences including conspiracy to murder (convictions for which had
been quashed by the Court of Appeal).

B. SPECIAL CASES

(c) Protectors, trustees and beneficiaries

Add new paragraph at end:

For an example of a request under the Data Protection Act 1998 by 4.26
beneficiaries against solicitors for trusts, see *Dawson-Damer v Taylor Wessing LLP* [2017] EWCA Civ 74, [2017] 1 W.L.R. 3255, CA.

Add new paragraph at end:

In *Lewis v Tamplin* [2018] EWHC 777 (Ch) beneficiaries with fixed 4.27
shares under a trust sought pre-action disclosure under CPR r.31.16
against the trustees. They also brought a Part 8 claim against the trustees
for disclosure and other information on the basis of the obligation owed
by trustees to account to beneficiaries for their stewardship. Applying
Rosewood Trust v Schmidt [2003] 2 AC 709, it was held that the benefi-
ciary of a fixed transmissible interest would normally obtain the assistance of the court, absent special circumstances (at [41-42]). In that case
there were no special circumstances and the claimant beneficiaries sought

the information for the right reason, which was to hold the trustees to account, and thus to vindicate their own beneficial interests, by way of an action for breach of trust if necessary (at [43]). It was held that legal advice obtained by the trustees for the benefit of the trust should be disclosed to the beneficiaries. In contrast, legal advice provided to the trustees personally not paid for out of the trust assets remains privileged as against the beneficiaries (at [59]).

D. NON-PARTIES

Requirements for non-party disclosure

Add new paragraph at end:

4.65 In *Sarayiah v Royal & Sun Alliance plc*, 12 April 2018 unreported Ch D (Barling J), the court made an order requiring the defendant insurer to provide a copy of a recording of a telephone conversation between his sister and the insurer in relation to an insurance policy relevant to and necessary for a claim between the claimant and the sister.

CHAPTER 5

What Must be Disclosed

CHAPTER 5

What Must be Disclosed

B. SCOPE OF THE OBLIGATION

Standard Disclosure

Add new paragraph at end:

Standard disclosure is no longer regarded the default option. CPR r.31.5   **5.20**
means that the selection of the correct approach is something not governed
by a prima facie rule, but by the overriding objective to deal with cases justly
and at proportionate cost. Further, other options for obtaining information,
such as an order for further information, should be considered: *Magnesium
Elektron Ltd v Neo Chemicals & Oxides (Europe) Ltd* [2017] EWHC 2957
(Pat) at [101-2].

C. PARTICULAR INSTANCES

(d) Insurance, funding and legal aid

Add new paragraph at end:

In *The RBS Rights Issue Litigation* [2017] EWHC 463 (Ch), the defendants   **5.36**
sought disclosure of the claimants' commercial funders pursuant to the
courts' jurisdiction ancillary to CPR r.25.14, and details of any ATE insurance pursuant to the courts' case management powers under CPR
r.3.1(2)(m) in advance of a threatened application for security for costs
when the trial was imminent. The jurisdiction to grant disclosure about
third-party funders is clear (at [32]) and has been previously recognised in
Reeves v Sprecher [2007] EWHC 3226 at [23] and *Wall v Royal Bank of
Scotland* [2016] EWHC 2460 (Comm). However, the applicant must demonstrate that the putative application for security for costs is a real possibility on realistic grounds, and not one simply posited as a possibility for some
tactical purpose without any real intention of pursuing it (at [35]). Further,
such an application must be demonstrated to have at least a realistic

prospect of success (at [36]). The court's case management powers under CPR r.3.1 extend to requiring disclosure of an ATE policy when its disclosure is necessary to enable the court proportionately and effectively to exercise its case management powers (at [104]). ATE policies are not by their nature privileged, but a disclosure order may permit certain information to be redacted (e.g. premium) if that would indicate legal advice on the merits of the dispute (at [112]).

D. SPECIAL CASES

(d) Terrorism

Add new paragraph at end:

5.54   For an example of an application under CPR rr.79.25-26 by HM Treasury to withhold from disclosure certain closed material on which it relied in defence of a claim, see *Bank Mellat v HM Treasury* [2017] EWHC 2931 (Admin). The matter was dealt with at a closed hearing (at which the claimant bank was not present or represented) submissions were made by both the defendant and a Special Advocate appointed for that purpose. The court applied the principles relating to the disclosure of closed material set out by the House of Lords in *Secretary of State for the Home Department v AF (No.3)* [2009] UKHL 28, [2010] 2 AC 269. The duty of disclosure in proceedings to set aside a financial restrictions decision under s.62 of the Counter-Terrorism Act 2008 relates to disclosure of allegations, not of evidence; the standard of disclosure is a relatively high one, and where detail matters, detail must be met with detail, and there must be a real opportunity for rebuttal (at [26]), applying *Bank Mellat v HM Treasury (No.4)* [2015] EWCA Civ 1052, [2016] 1 W.L.R. 1187 at [33–35].

E. "POSSESSION, CUSTODY OR POWER"/"CONTROL"

Possession

Add new paragraph at end:

5.61   Solicitors' working papers belong to the firm and not its client. Hence the client has no right to delivery up or disclosure: *Green v SGI Legal LLP*, 18 December 2017, Master Leonard (unreported). In that case the Master rejected an application for delivery up of papers under s.68(1) of the Solicitors Act 1974. This does not preclude disclosure in the context of a pre-action disclosure application under CPR r.31.16. See also *Whale v Mooney Everett Solicitors*, 12 June 2018 unreported, SCCO (Master Leonard).

CHAPTER 6

Means of Disclosure

CHAPTER 6

Means of Disclosure

A. LISTS OF DOCUMENTS

Correction of errors

Add new paragraph at end:

In *Atlantirealm Ltd v Intelligent Land Investments (Renewable Energy) Ltd* **6.29**
[2017] EWCA Civ 1029, [2018] 4 W.L.R. 6, CA, a junior lawyer disclosed
a privileged email by mistake. The claimant was restrained from using the
document as the disclosure was an obvious mistake, hence had been inad-
vertently disclosed within the meaning of CPR r.31.20. It was noted that in
the electronic age disclosure can be a massive and expensive exercise, where
mistakes will occur from time to time. If mistakes are obvious, the lawyers
on both sides should co-operate to put matters right as soon as possible (at
[55]). The Court of Appeal applied the principles set out in *Al-Fayed v
Commissioner of Police of the Metropolis* [2002] EWCA Civ 780 at [16]
and *Rawlinson and Hunter Trustees SA v Director of the Serious Fraud
Office (No.2)* [2014] EWCA Civ 1129, [2015] 1 W.L.R. 797 at [15]. The
principles in *Al-Fayed* were qualified to cover the situation where the
inspecting solicitor does not spot the mistake but refers the document to a
more percipient colleague who does spot the mistake before us is made of
the document, then the court may grant relief on the basis that has become
a case of obvious mistake (at [68]).

At the end of fn.106 add:

[106] In *Lachaux v Independent Print Ltd* [2017] EWCA Civ 1327, [2018] EMLR 2, the Court **6.32**
of Appeal dismissed an appeal from [2015] EWHC 3677 (QB). The judge was correct to grant
an injunction preventing use and ordering the return of privileged advice to the claimant. The
documents had been obtained by the defendant from the claimant's computer without his
consent. It was held that the emergence of the truth from the documents was not sufficient to
override the privilege or from the basis of refusing the relief sought.

Add new paragraph at end:

Following the principles set out in *Al Fayed v Commissioner of Police of the* **6.33**
Metropolis [2002] EWCA Civ 780 at [16], in general permission under CPR

r.31.20 to use privileged documents disclosed by mistake, will usually be refused if the solicitor provided the documents appreciates that a mistake has been made before making some use of the documents (para.(vii)(a)). In *Single Buoy Mooring Inc v Aspen Insurance Ltd* [2018] EWHC 1763 (Comm), Teare J considered what "use" means in this context. He rejected an argument that it is confined to tendered in evidence (at [15]). He also considered that it would be a too narrow interpretation to confine it to tendered in evidence, or deployed in a letter, pleading or statement. He held that where documents had been provided under early disclosure by the claimant's solicitors who invited defendant's solicitor to read them, and he did read them, then that would amount to use (at [16]).

E. CONCLUSIVENESS OF LIST OR AFFIDAVIT

At the end of fn.144 add:

6.45   [144] In *Single Buoy Moorings Inc v Aspen Insurance UK Ltd* [2018] EWHC 1763 (Comm), the principles set out in *West London Pipeline and Storage Ltd v Total UK Ltd* [2016] 1 W.L.R. 361 at [13] was applied. In *Single Buoy* the Court went behind a solicitor's claim to privilege as it was evident that the claim had been made on an erroneous basis (at [31]).

F. APPLICATION FOR SPECIFIC DISCLOSURE

Add new paragraphs at end:

6.48   In *Lisle-Mainwaring v Associated Newspapers Ltd* [2018] EWCA Civ 1470, Coulson LJ (with whom Newey LJ agreed) set out CPR r.31.12, and continued:

"34. Thus, in my judgment, the rules are intended to operate in this way:
 a) Where there is an order for standard disclosure, each party has to list those documents which arise in the three sub-categories of r.31.6(b). As the notes to the White Book make plain, whether or not a document falls into these sub-paragraphs must be judged against the statements of case, and not by reference to other matters: see *Paddick v Associated Newspapers Limited* [2003] EWHC 2991 (QB); [2003] All ER (D) 179 (Dec) at [11].
 b) After receipt of the other side's list, a party may conclude that it wishes to seek specific disclosure of particular documents or classes of documents. If so, an application is made under r.31.12. The court has a discretion as to whether or not to grant such an order.
 c) The application for specific disclosure will usually arise because the applicant believes that the other party has not given adequate

disclosure first time round. But that is not inevitable: sometimes, there may be documents (or a particular class of documents) which the applicant seeks by way of specific disclosure, regardless of whether or not they should have been disclosed by way of standard disclosure.

35. The fact that an application for specific disclosure can be made in either circumstance is clear from Practice Direction 31A, where the relevant provisions are as follows:

'Specific disclosure

5.1 If a party believes that the disclosure of documents given by a disclosing party is inadequate he may make an application for an order for specific disclosure (see rule 31.12).

5.2 The application notice must specify the order that the applicant intends to ask the court to make and must be supported by evidence (see rule 31.12(2) which describes the orders the court may make).

5.3 The grounds on which the order is sought may be set out in the application notice itself but if not there set out must be set out in the evidence filed in support of the application.

5.4 In deciding whether or not to make an order for specific disclosure the court will take into account all the circumstances of the case and, in particular, the overriding objective described in Part 1. But if the court concludes that the party from whom specific disclosure is sought has failed adequately to comply with the obligations imposed by an order for disclosure (whether by failing to make a sufficient search for documents or otherwise) the court will usually make such order as is necessary to ensure that those obligations are properly complied with.

5.5 An order for specific disclosure may in an appropriate case direct a party to—

(1) carry out a search for any documents which it is reasonable to suppose may contain information which may–
(a) enable the party applying for disclosure either to advance his own case or to damage that of the party giving disclosure; or
(b) lead to a train of enquiry which has either of those consequences; and

(2) disclose any documents found as a result of that search.'

36. Thus, if a court concluded that the respondent to the application had failed to comply with the order for standard disclosure, then it will "usually" make the appropriate order: see paragraph 5.4 of PD 31A. If, on the other hand, the court is not so persuaded, then it may be more

difficult for the applicant to obtain an order for specific disclosure. But it is not impossible. That is because, as paragraph 5.5(1) makes clear, in an appropriate case, the court may make an order for disclosure which is wider than the constraints governing standard disclosure and could even extend to an old-fashioned 'train of enquiry' exercise (the unlamented *Peruvian Guano* test). An order made pursuant to paragraph 5.5(1)(b) of Practice Direction 31 could never arise out of a failure to comply with an order for specific disclosure, and would only be justified in an appropriate case.

37. For these reasons, therefore, it seems to me that the interface between standard disclosure and specific disclosure is clear. It gives rise to no difficulties in practice or principle."

CHAPTER 10

Production by Non-Parties

CHAPTER 10

Production by Non-Parties

D. EVIDENCE (PROCEEDINGS IN OTHER JURISDICTIONS) ACT 1975

Limitations imposed by the Act

Add new paragraph at end:

In *Allergen Inc v Amazon Medica* [2018] EWHC 307 (QB), the court set **10.55** aside an Order made under the Evidence (Proceedings in Other Jurisdictions) Act 1975 pursuant to a letter of request issued by a US Court. The letter of request was for oral testimony and documents were found to be too wide and not for trial, but in effect, it was seeking disclosure as part of the pre-trial investigatory process. The court is not bound to accept the assertions in a letter of request that the material is sought for the purposes of trial (at [56]). In deciding jurisdiction, the key points are questions of relevance and intention to use at trial. Cockerill J was of the view that admissibility is rarely of relevance in the context of a letter of request (at [55]).

CHAPTER 11

Objections to Inspection (1): Introduction and Legal Professional Privilege

CHAPTER 11

Objections to Inspection (1): Introduction and Legal Professional Privilege

C. LEGAL PROFESSIONAL PRIVILEGE

At the end of fn.26 add:

26 See also *Director of the Serious Fraud Office v Eurasian Natural Resources Ltd* [2018] **11.05**
EWCA Civ 2006, [63].

At the end of fn.29 add:

29 See also *Property Alliance Ltd v Royal Bank of Scotland plc* [2016] 1 W.L.R. 992, [44]–[45]; **11.05**
Director of the Serious Fraud Office v Eurasian Natural Resources Ltd [2017] EWHC 1017
(QB), [67] (reversed on other grounds [2018] EWCA Civ 2006).

At the end of fn.43 add:

43 The decision in *Shlosberg v Avonwick Holdings Ltd* [2016] EWHC 1001 (Ch) was affirmed **11.07**
by the Court of Appeal sub nom *Avonwick Holdings Ltd v Shlosberg* [2016] EWCA Civ 1158,
[2017] 2 W.L.R. 1075. However, the Court of Appeal's reasoning was different: see in
particular at [53]–[64], where Sir Terence Etherton MR held that the mere width of the
definition of property in the legislation was not sufficiently express to deprive the bankrupt of
his privilege.

At the end of fn.44 add:

44 The decision in *Shlosberg v Avonwick Holdings Ltd* [2016] EWHC 1001 (Ch) was affirmed **11.07**
by the Court of Appeal sub nom *Avonwick Holdings Ltd v Shlosberg* [2016] EWCA Civ 1158,
[2017] 2 W.L.R. 1075. However, the Court of Appeal's reasoning was different: see in
particular at [53]–[64], where Sir Terence Etherton MR held that the mere width of the
definition of property in the legislation was not sufficiently express to deprive the bankrupt of
his privilege. See also *Leeds v Lemos* [2018] Ch 81, holding that LPP remains with the
bankrupt, who cannot be required to waive it.

At the end of fn.45 add:

45 The decision in *Shlosberg v Avonwick Holdings Ltd* [2016] EWHC 1001 (Ch) was affirmed **11.07**
by the Court of Appeal sub nom *Avonwick Holdings Ltd v Shlosberg* [2016] EWCA Civ 1158,
[2017] 2 W.L.R. 1075. However, the Court of Appeal's reasoning was different: see in

particular at [53]–[64], where Sir Terence Etherton MR held that the mere width of the definition of property in the legislation was not sufficiently express to deprive the bankrupt of his privilege.

At the end of fn.47 add:

[47] This was followed in *Addlesee v Dentons Europe LLP* [2018] EWHC 3010 (Ch).

At the end of fn.61 add:

11.09 [61] See also *Director of the Serious Fraud Office v Eurasian Natural Resources Ltd* [2017] EWHC 1017 (QB), [37] (reversed on other grounds [2018] EWCA Civ 2006); *The Financial Reporting Council v Sports Direct International Ltd* [2018] EWHC 2282 (Ch), [58].

At the end of fn.62 add:

11.09 [62] See *The Financial Reporting Council v Sports Direct International Ltd* [2018] EWHC 2282 (Ch), [58].

At the end of fn.64 add:

11.10 [64] See also *Edwards-Tubb v JD Wetherspoon PLC* [2011] 1 W.L.R. 1373, CA; *Lalana Hans Place Ltd v Michael Barclay Partnership LLP* [2017] EWHC 29 (TCC), [21].

D. LEGAL ADVICE PRIVILEGE

The basic rule

At the end of fn.80 add:

11.11 [80] In *Director of the Serious Fraud Office v Eurasian Natural Resources Ltd* [2018] EWCA Civ 2006, [132], the Court of Appeal considered provisionally that (in contrast with litigation privilege) there was no basis for saying that the dominant purpose of supplying information to the lawyer was to obtain legal advice.

At the end of fn.82 add:

11.11 [82] See also *Director of the Serious Fraud Office v Eurasian Natural Resources Ltd* [2018] EWCA Civ 2006, [65]; *cf The Financial Reporting Council v Sports Direct International Ltd* [2018] EWHC 2282 (Ch), [35] (the mere fact that pre-existing documents are attached to emails passing between client and lawyer does not render those documents privileged).

At the end of fn.94 add:

11.12 [94] See also *Kerman v Akhmedova* [2018] 4 W.L.R. 52, CA, [43], [45]–[47].

Add new paragraph at end:

11.14 It is clear that for this purpose communications include documents which *evidence* the substance of such communications: *Three Rivers District Council v Bank of England (No 5)* [2003] QB 1556, [19], [21]; *Re Edwardian Group Ltd, Estera Trust (Jersey) Ltd v Singh* [2017] EWHC 2805

(Ch), [28]. In this context, "evidences" means that there must be "a definite and reasonable foundation in the contents of the document for the suggested inference as to the substance of the legal advice given", rather than "merely something which would allow one to wonder or speculate whether legal advice had been obtained and as to the substance of that advice": *Re Edwardian Group Ltd, Estera Trust (Jersey) Ltd v Singh* [2017] EWHC 2805 (Ch), [37]. It has also been held that lawyers' *working papers* are treated for the purposes of legal advice privilege as equivalent to communications to the extent that they would betray the tenor of communicated advice: see *The RBS Rights Litigation* [2016] EWHC 3161 (Ch), [99]–[107]; *Director of the Serious Fraud Office v Eurasian Natural Resources Ltd* [2017] EWHC 1017 (QB), [95]–[97] (reversed on other grounds [2018] EWCA Civ 2006; at [142] the Court of Appeal declined to express a view).

At the end of fn.107 add:

107 See also *McCallum-Toppin v McCallum-Toppin*, unreported 20 June 2018, Fancourt J **11.14** (solicitors' timesheets might be redacted to exclude references to subject-matter of work done, but were otherwise not privileged).

At the end of fn.117 add:

117 See also *Director of the Serious Fraud Office v Eurasian Natural Resources Ltd* [2017] **11.15** EWHC 1017 (QB), [178] (reversed on other grounds [2018] EWCA Civ 2006).

Third parties

At the end of fn.129 add:

129 See also *Kerman v Akhmedova* [2018] 4 W.L.R. 52, CA, [48]–[51]. **11.17**

Add new paragraphs at end:

The decision of the Court of Appeal in *Three Rivers District Council v Bank* **11.19** *of England (No 5)* [2003] QB 1556 was followed by Hildyard J in *The RBS Rights Litigation* [2016] EWHC 3161 (Ch) and by Andrews J in *Director of the Serious Fraud Office v Eurasian Natural Resources Ltd* [2017] EWHC 1017 (QB), [68]–[93] (and see also *Astex Therapeutics v AstraZeneca AB* [2016] EWHC 2759 (Ch) (Chief Master Marsh)). The Court of Appeal ([2018] EWCA Civ 2006, [133]), though reversing her decision on other grounds, affirmed Andrews J on this point, indicating that it too would have felt obliged to follow *Three Rivers District Council v Bank of England (No 5)*. However, that court also indicated that, if it had been open to it to do so, it would have been in favour of departing from that decision.

The Court of Appeal said ([2018] EWCA Civ 2006):

"125. First, we do not think that a meticulous analysis of the 19th century authorities should be determinative, because, in our judgment, those cases were decided when the distinction between litigation privilege and legal advice privilege was very much in its infancy. It is more important that a principled analysis of the purpose of legal advice privilege should be undertaken. Lord Scott in *Three Rivers (No. 6)* set out the parameters as follows at paragraphs 28–30 . . .

126. Lord Scott also referred to passages to a similar effect in *B v Auckland District Law Society* [2003] 2 AC 736 at paragraph 47 per Lord Millett, in *Upjohn Co v United States* (1981) 449 US 383 per Justice Rehnquist in the US Supreme Court, in *Jones v Smith* [1999] 1 SCR 455 per the Supreme Court of Canada at pages 474–475, in *Baker v Campbell* (1983) 153 CLR 52 per Murphy J and Wilson J in the High Court of Australia at pages 89 and 95 respectively, in *Commissioner of Inland Revenue v West-Walker* [1954] NZLR 191, and in *A M & S Europe Ltd v Commission of the European Communities* (Case 155/79) [1983] QB 878 at page 913 per Advocate General Slynn. He then concluded his section on the rationale for legal advice privilege with the following at paragraph 34 . . .

127. This last passage makes clear that large corporations need, as much as small corporations and individuals, to seek and obtain legal advice without fear of intrusion. If legal advice privilege is confined to communications passing between the lawyer and the 'client' (in the sense of the instructing individual or those employees of a company authorised to seek and receive legal advice on its behalf), this presents no problem for individuals and many small businesses, since the information about the case will normally be obtained by the lawyer from the individual or board members of the small corporation. That was the position in most of the 19th century cases. In the modern world, however, we have to cater for legal advice sought by large national corporations and indeed multinational ones. In such cases, the information upon which legal advice is sought is unlikely to be in the hands of the main board or those it appoints to seek and receive legal advice. If a multi-national corporation cannot ask its lawyers to obtain the information it needs to advise that corporation from the corporation's employees with relevant first-hand knowledge under the protection of legal advice privilege, that corporation will be in a less advantageous position than a smaller entity seeking such advice. In our view, at least, whatever the rule is, it should be equally applicable to all clients, whatever their size or reach. Moreover, it is not always an answer to say that the relevant subsidiary can seek the necessary legal advice and, therefore, ask its own lawyers to secure the necessary information with the protection of legal advice privilege. In a case such as the present, there may be issues between group companies that

make it desirable for the parent company to be able to procure the information necessary to obtain its own legal advice.

128. We were referred specifically in this connection to a decision of the Singapore Court of Appeal in the *Enskilda Bank* case, where Andrew Phang Boon Leong JA held at paragraphs 41–42 that the *ratio* of *Three Rivers (No. 5)* was that only the BIU was authorised to communicate with the bank's lawyers, and that 'since a company can only act through its employees, communications made by [authorised employees] would be communications "made on behalf of the client", and can attract legal advice privilege'. In addition, in *Citic Pacific Ltd v Secretary for Justice* [2016] 1 HKC 157, the Hong Kong Court of Appeal (Lam VP, Barma JA and Poon J) concluded that a dominant purpose test in legal advice privilege was to be preferred to the narrow definition of the "client" adopted in *Three Rivers (No. 5)* (see paragraphs 39–56 in the judgment of the court, and paragraphs 53–55 in the context of large corporations).

129. Finally in this connection, it seems to us, as Ms Rose submitted on behalf of the Law Society, that English law is out of step with the international common law on this issue. It is undoubtedly desirable for the common law in different countries to remain aligned so far as its development is not specifically affected by different commercial or cultural environments in those countries. In this regard, legal professional privilege is a classic example of an area where one might expect to see commonality between the laws of common law countries, particularly when so many multinational companies operate across borders and have subsidiaries in numerous common law countries.

130. If, therefore, it had been open to us to depart from *Three Rivers (No. 5)*, we would have been in favour of doing so. For the reasons we have given, however, we do not think that it is open to us, so it is a matter that will have to be considered again by the Supreme Court in this or an appropriate future case."

However, the Court of Appeal was clear that ex-employees were to be treated as third parties for the purposes of legal advice privilege, which could not, therefore, attach anyway:

"139. In our judgment, information obtained from ex-employees falls into the same category as that obtained from third parties, which ENRC accepts cannot be held to be covered by legal advice privilege at this level. An ex-employee is in all respects equivalent to a third party, and however desirable it might be that information obtained from such a person should be covered by legal advice privilege, we do not think that that is, on any analysis, the current law. As the SFO submitted, the only authority emanates from the USA, where there are two cases pointing in different directions."

At the end of fn.147, add:

¹⁴⁷ See *Glaxo Wellcome UK Ltd v Sandoz Ltd* [2018] EWHC 2747 Ch, [17]–[21].

What kind of lawyer?

At the end of fn.161 add:

11.23   ¹⁶¹ See also *The Financial Reporting Council v Sports Direct International Ltd* [2018] EWHC 2282 (Ch), [29].

Confidentiality

Add new paragraph at end:

11.32   In *Simpkin v The Berkeley Group plc* [2017] 4 W.L.R. 116, [29]–[42], Garnham J held that a document created by the claimant on his employer's computer at work, stored on its server, and sent by him over the employer's email system to his private email address, was not confidential as against the employer and hence could not be privileged as against it.

E. LITIGATION PRIVILEGE

The basic rule

Add new paragraphs at end:

11.35   In *Minera Las Bambas SA v Glencore Queensland Ltd* [2018] EWHC 286 (Comm), Moulder J held that a person exercising a contractual right to conduct (foreign) litigation in the name of another was not entitled as against that other to claim litigation privilege in communications made to it for the dominant purpose of that litigation. The judge rejected the submission (at [18]) that:

> "*Guinness Peat Properties Ltd and another v Fitzroy Robinson Partnership* [1987] 1 WLR 1027 is authority for the proposition that in a case in which a person is '*in all but name the effective defendant to the proceedings*' the privilege will belong to that person."

Moulder J said:

> "31. Counsel for the Defendants suggests that the fact that Slade LJ (sitting in the Court of Appeal) was willing to depart from a decision of the House of Lords in *Jones* because '*the insurers will in all but name be*

the effective defendants to any proceedings' meant that it formed part of the *ratio* of the decision of the Court of Appeal in *Guinness Peat* and it was, therefore, binding on me in this case in which the Defendants are *'in all but name'* a party to the Peruvian Proceedings. However, in my view, it is not authority for the proposition that a person controlling litigation can assert litigation privilege against the party which it is controlling and who is the party to the proceedings. I accept the Claimants' submission that it is an established principle that litigation privilege can only arise in favour of a person who is a party to the litigation in question and the policy underlying this is as stated in *Hollander* (12th edition para 18−01) that a party should be free to seek evidence without being obliged to disclose the results to the other side. This rationale does not extend to a non-party. Accordingly, I find that any right to assert litigation privilege arising out of the Peruvian Proceedings is that of the Claimants as a party to those proceedings and, it is not open to the Defendants to assert such privilege against them."

Add new paragraph at end:

Brown v Alexander, 30 July 2018 unreported QBD (HHJ Graham Wood **11.35**
QC), concerned a personal injury claim. The defendant's insurers funded a rehabilitation scheme (pursuant to the Pre-Action Protocol) for the claimant, who had suffered brain damage in the accident the subject of the claim. Although the immediate needs assessment was held covered by litigation privilege, progress reports issued under the scheme thereafter were not.

At the end of fn.224 add:

[224] See also *Director of the Serious Fraud Office v Eurasian Natural Resources Ltd* [2018] **11.35**
EWCA Civ 2006, [64].

Add new paragraphs at end:

In *Director of the Serious Fraud Office v Eurasian Natural Resources Ltd* **11.36**
[2018] EWCA Civ 2006, the Court of Appeal said:

"102. [. . .] The fact that solicitors prepare a document with the ultimate intention of showing that document to the opposing party does not, in our judgment, automatically deprive the preparatory legal work that they have undertaken of litigation privilege. We can imagine many circumstances where solicitors may spend much time fine-tuning a response to a claim in order to give their client the best chance of reaching an early settlement. The discussions surrounding the drafting of such a letter would be as much covered by litigation privilege as any other work done in preparing to defend the claim. [. . .] In both the civil and the criminal context, legal advice given so as to head off, avoid or even settle reasonably contemplated proceedings is as much protected by litigation privilege as advice given for the purpose of resisting or defending such contemplated proceedings."

Copies

At the end of fn.249 add:

11.38   249 See also *The Financial Reporting Council v Sports Direct International Ltd* [2018] EWHC 2282 (Ch), [31]–[42]. *Cf Director of the Serious Fraud Office v Eurasian Natural Resources Ltd* [2017] EWHC 1017 (QB), [182] (reversed on other grounds [2018] EWCA Civ 2006).

What is "ligitation"?

At the end of fn.264 add:

11.41   264 See also *Smith v SWM Ltd* [2017] JRC 026 (report requested and supplied to the regulator; held not covered by litigation privilege).

When is litigation contemplated?

Add new paragraphs at end:

11.43   In *Director of the Serious Fraud Office v Eurasian Natural Resources Ltd* [2018] EWCA Civ 2006, the question in civil proceedings was whether documents were privileged because brought into existence in contemplation of other, criminal proceedings. The Court of Appeal said:

> "92. The contemporaneous documents do not, as the judge suggested, show that ENRC failed at the first hurdle of showing that, as at 19th August 2011, it was "aware of circumstances which rendered litigation between itself and the SFO a real likelihood rather than a mere possibility" (adopting the test in [*United States of America v Philip Morris Inc* [2003] EWHC 3028 (Comm)]). Those documents demonstrate, we think, the reverse. [. . .]
>
> 93. In these circumstances, it seems to us that the whole sub-text of the relationship between ENRC and the SFO was the possibility, if not the likelihood, of prosecution if the self-reporting process did not result in a civil settlement. [. . .]
>
> 94. Andrews J may have been justified in thinking that the process was at an early stage triggered simply by the whistle-blower email and the press allegations relating to Camrose, but that did not mean that the SFO

was not taking a serious and concerted interest in ENRC's activities in Kazakhstan and Africa.

95. We accept also that Mr Gerrard's view was not conclusive, and he may have wanted to create a situation where legal professional privilege covered what he was doing, but that again does not mean that a criminal prosecution was not actually in contemplation.

96. As regards ENRC's first legal point under this heading, we are not sure that every SFO manifestation of concern would properly be regarded as adversarial litigation, but when the SFO specifically makes clear to the company the prospect of its criminal prosecution (over and above the general principles set out in the Guidelines), and legal advisers are engaged to deal with that situation, as in the present case, there is a clear ground for contending that criminal prosecution is in reasonable contemplation.

97. Secondly, we do not think that Etherton LJ's *dicta* in [*Westminster International BV v Dornoch* [2009] EWCA Civ 1323] lead inevitably to the conclusion that once an SFO criminal investigation is reasonably in contemplation, so too is a criminal prosecution. As Etherton LJ concluded at paragraph 36 of *Dornoch*: "[e]ach case turns on its own facts and will be judged in the light of the facts as a whole. Neither a statement on behalf of the insurer as to its state of mind, nor the mere fact of retaining solicitors, will separately or together necessarily be sufficient to satisfy the requirements for litigation privilege". Here, however, the documents and evidence pointed clearly towards the contemplation of a prosecution if the self-reporting process did not succeed in averting it.

98. Thirdly, whilst a party anticipating possible prosecution will often need to make further investigations before it can say with certainty that proceedings are likely, that uncertainty, in our judgment, does not in itself prevent proceedings being in reasonable contemplation. In the present case, the uncertainty was a function of ENRC not having the information required to evaluate the whistle-blower email or the Camrose issues. An individual suspected of a crime will, of course, know whether he has committed it. An international corporation will be in a different position, but the fact that there is uncertainty does not mean that, in colloquial terms, the writing may not be clearly written on the wall. We think the judge was wrong to regard the uncertainty as pointing against a real likelihood of a prosecution. The reasoning in paragraphs 162–163 of her judgment could not outweigh the clear indications of a likely prosecution contained in the documents to which we have referred.

99. The judge's distinction between civil and criminal proceedings was, in our judgment, illusory. Of course, civil proceedings are sometimes brought without foundation, but here there was no suggestion that the threat of criminal prosecution was anything other than extremely serious. We are conscious, in this connection, of two matters in particular. First, the Bribery Act 2010 was not actually in force at the relevant time, and

secondly, that difficulties may arise in prosecutions in respect of conduct undertaken overseas. Despite these factors, ENRC was actually being told in this case that, if it did not cooperate and allow its professional advisers to undertake an investigation, prosecution would be even more likely. It would be wrong for it to be thought that, in a criminal context, a potential defendant is likely to be denied the benefit of litigation privilege when he asks his solicitor to investigate the circumstances of any alleged offence.

100. [. . .] For the reasons we have given, Andrews J was not right to suggest a general principle that litigation privilege cannot attach until either a defendant knows the full details of what is likely to be unearthed or a decision to prosecute has been taken. The fact that a formal investigation has not commenced will be one part of the factual matrix, but will not necessarily be determinative.

101. In these circumstances, we would allow ENRC's appeal against the judge's finding that, at no stage before all the Documents had been created, criminal legal proceedings against ENRC or its subsidiaries or their employees were reasonably in its contemplation. It seems to us that ENRC was right to say that they were in reasonable contemplation when it initiated its investigation in April 2011, and certainly by the time it received the SFO's August 2011 letter."

Cf R v Jukes [2018] Cr.App.R 9, where a company director gave a statement to the company's solicitor during an investigatory phase after an industrial accident, and the statement was held not to be made in contemplation of litigation (but the court referred to the decision at first instance in *ENRC*, later overturned by the Court of Appeal, above).

At the end of fn.283 add:

11.43   [283] See also *Director of the Serious Fraud Office v Eurasian Natural Resources Ltd* [2018] EWCA Civ 2006 (actual civil litigation and contemplated criminal litigation).

The question of purpose

Add new paragraph at end:

11.50   In considering whether a document is privileged, the question of the purpose for which it was created is a question of fact (*Director of the Serious Fraud Office v Eurasian Natural Resources Ltd* [2018] EWCA Civ 2006, [104]), which will make it harder to obtain permission to appeal the decision: *Bilta (UK) Ltd v Royal Bank of Scotland plc* [2017] 1 W.L.R. 3630, [59], [74] (solicitors' report prepared to resist expected tax assessment by HMRC held privileged; *Director of the Serious Fraud Office v Eurasian Natural Resources Ltd* [2017] EWHC 1017 (QB) distinguished).

At the end of fn.319 add:

³¹⁹ In considering the question of purpose, "use" in litigation is not confined to admission as evidence, but extends to use to resist, avoid or settle proceedings (*Re Highgrade Traders* [1984] BCLC 151, CA; *Bilta (UK) Ltd v Royal Bank of Scotland plc* [2017] 1 W.L.R 3630; *Director of the Serious Fraud Office v Eurasian Natural Resources Ltd* [2018] EWCA Civ 2006, [113]; *cf Bailey v Beagle Management Pty* [2001] FCA 185, [11]).   **11.50**

At the end of fn.328 add:

³²⁸ See also *Smith v SWM Ltd* [2017] JRC 026 (report requested and supplied to regulator; held not covered by litigation privilege).   **11.51**

At the end of fn.342 add:

³⁴² See also *Minera Las Bambas SA v Glencore Queensland Ltd* [2018] EWHC 286 (Comm), [38].   **11.54**

At the end of fn.343 add:

³⁴³ See also *Westminster International BV v Dornoch* [2009] EWCA Civ 1323, [36]; *Director of the Serious Fraud Office v Eurasian Natural Resources Ltd* [2017] EWHC 1017 (QB), [38].   **11.54**

Communications between persons with a "common interest"

At the end of fn.406 add:

⁴⁰⁶ See also *Accident Exchange Ltd v MacLean* [2018] 4 W.L.R 26, [77].   **11.67**

F. EXCEPTIONS TO LEGAL PROFESSIONAL PRIVILEGE

(c) Fraud or illegality

At the end of fn.462 add:

⁴⁶² See also *Accident Exchange Ltd v MacLean* [2018] 4 W.L.R. 26, [15]–[18].   **11.76**

Add new paragraphs at end:

In *Accident Exchange Ltd v MacLean* [2018] 4 W.L.R. 26, it was argued that the defendant motorists' legal privilege in communications with their solicitors was taken away by the fact that a third party engaged by the   **11.78** solicitors' insurers to provide evidence of hire charges gave false evidence in other litigation. Sir Andrew Smith said:

"47. As I have said, Mr Adam (and Mr Hough, who adopted Mr Adam's arguments) argued that in third party iniquity cases the iniquity exception applies only if the wrongdoer's iniquity is 'upstream' of the solicitor/client relationship, so as to bring it about. I can accept that this might be the hallmark of a typical case in which the law, as developed in *Francis and Francis*, applies, but again I think that Mr Adam goes too far: I cannot accept that there is an acid test of this kind as to when third party wrongdoing will override privilege, and I have already observed (at para 31) that this submission does not sit readily with the judgment in the *Kamal XXVI* case (loc cit). Nor, for example, can I believe that the result in the *Francis and Francis* case would have been different if Mrs G had already been instructing the solicitors to buy a modest property, her relative provided funds by way of drug trafficking to buy a mansion instead, and Mrs G changed the instructions to the solicitors accordingly.

48. As in cases of iniquity on the part of a lawyer's client it is, as Popplewell J [in *JSC BTA Bank v Ablyazov*] concluded, a question of fact and degree whether the iniquity takes the lawyer/client relationship outside the ordinary scope of professional employment, in my judgment it is a question of fact and degree whether the nexus between the wrongdoer and client does so. This might be said to be an unsatisfactorily vague test for determining whether a client enjoys legal professional privilege, but Popplewell J's compelling analysis of cases of client iniquity in *JSC BTA Bank v Ablyazov* (loc cit) led him to a conclusion of which the same criticism might be made. And indeed, that is the basis on which Lord Bridge criticised the test enunciated by Lord Goff.

49. Approaching the issue on this basis, I conclude that the documents of which AE seeks inspection are protected by privilege, and that the iniquity exception does not apply to them. The essential considerations can be shortly stated: in the cases in which third party iniquity has deprived an innocent client of the protection of privilege, the wrongdoer and the client have had a relationship (or nexus) separate from the dealings with a solicitor, and that separate relationship was used by the wrongdoer to advance the wrongdoing. In my judgment, such connections between client and wrongdoer and between their relationship and the iniquity will be a hallmark of cases where an innocent client loses the protection of privilege. They might not be absolute requirements in all such cases, but I find it difficult to envisage a case in which they would not be present. This case is very different: AF's wrongdoing was properly described by Mr Adam as "parasitic" upon an existing lawyer/client relationship, which was created and continued for a normal and legitimate purpose. I accept the arguments of Mr Adam and Mr Hough that AF has not used the defendant drivers or their underwriters as its tool, nor has it done anything

that might mean that their relationship with the defendant solicitors is not of the ordinary kind. To apply the iniquity exception to this case would be a major innovation that I consider unjustified by authority, legal principle or established principles of public policy."

At the end of fn.467 add:

[467] See also *Accident Exchange Ltd v MacLean* [2018] 4 W.L.R. 26, [19]–[21], [23]–[24]. **11.78**

At the end of fn.468 add:

[468] See also *Accident Exchange Ltd v MacLean* [2018] 4 W.L.R 26, [19]–[22]. **11.78**

At the end of fn.476 add:

[476] See also *BGBP Managing Global Partner Ltd v Babcock & Brown Global Partners* [2011] Ch 296, [68]; *Holyoake v Candy* [2017] EWHC 52 (Ch), [76]. **11.79**

At the end of fn.485 add:

[485] See also *Holyoake v Candy* [2017] EWHC 52 (Ch), [76]. **11.79**

Add new paragraphs at end:

The exception for fraud or illegality does not extend to breaches of funda- **11.80** mental human rights. In *Holyoake v Candy* [2017] EWHC 52 (Ch), Morgan J said:

"91. Having reached those conclusions [on the facts] I can deal relatively shortly with the points of law. The authorities relied on are of no real assistance to the argument. The words of Lord Hobhouse in *Morgan Grenfell* are of no help to Ms Proops, representing no more than a minority obiter comment in a case which faithfully applied established principles, as to which see below. The three cases relied on as indicating that 'iniquity' has a broader meaning than just crime or fraud are first instance authority on facts far removed from the present, and do nothing to support the broad submissions advanced. *Brown* was concerned with legal advice privilege not litigation privilege, and establishes a qualification of narrow scope based on quite exceptional facts (the point at issue was whether staff should be allowed to attend a conference between a convicted murderer and his lawyers to prevent the applicant committing suicide). It is true that the exception was rooted in a Convention right—the right to life. But I think it would be going much too far to treat this decision as a springboard for the much broader submission that the court is duty bound to allow an incursion into LPP whenever the documents for which protection is sought may evidence a breach of any human right.

92. That, on analysis, has to be the logic of Ms Proops' position. However much she may emphasise the 'fundamental' nature of the privacy rights at issue in this case she cannot submit that they fall into any

special or separate category from other fundamental human rights. If the argument is sound, it must apply to other human rights such as (for instance) the right to freedom of expression protected by Article 10, or the right to peaceful enjoyment of possessions protected by Article 1 of Protocol 1. It seems to me therefore that Mr Pitt-Payne is right to submit that this argument seeks a substantial expansion of the iniquity principle which would, on the face of it, significantly erode the right to LPP. I also see a great deal of force in Mr Pitt-Payne's submission that the argument for Mr Holyoake fails properly to recognise that the right to LPP is itself a fundamental human right. Authority establishes that LPP is an aspect of the rights protected by Article 8 ECHR (see *Campbell v United Kingdom* (1992) 15 EHRR 137). Those same rights are also protected by Article 7 of the Charter. Recognition of the need in the public interest to protect communications between client and lawyer is a common feature of European legal systems so that the protection of LPP is, to some extent at least, a principle of EU law: *A M & S Europe Ltd v Commission of the European Communities* (Case 155/79) [1983] QB 878 [21–22]."

At the end of fn.486 add:

11.80 [486] See also *Kerman v Akhmedova* [2018] 4 W.L.R. 52, CA, [44], [54]–[57].

At the end of fn.503 add:

11.81 [503] See also *Holyoake v Candy* [2017] EWHC 52 (Ch), [77].

(d) As between trustee (or personal representative) and beneficiary, or partnership and partner

At the end of fn.513 add:

11.86 [513] See also *Dawson-Damer v Taylor Wessing LLP* [2017] 1 W.L.R. 3255, CA (LPP exception in Data Protection Act 1998, Sch.7 para.10 restricted to LPP under law of any part of UK).

Amend the case name at fn.515:

11.86 [515] The reference to *Birseye* should read *Birdseye*.

"Joint interest" privilege

At the end of fn.525 add:

11.91 [525] See also *Accident Exchange Ltd v MacLean* [2018] 4 W.L.R. 26, [76].

(f) Joint clients

At the end of fn.526 add:

11.92 [526] The decision in *Shlosberg v Avonwick Holdings Ltd* [2016] EWHC 1001 (Ch) was affirmed by the Court of Appeal sub nom *Avonwick Holdings Ltd v Shlosberg* [2016] EWCA Civ 1158, [2017] 2 W.L.R. 1075. See especially at [91]–[92].

(h) Secondary evidence available

At the end of fn.533 add:

[533] See also *Lachaux v Independent Print Ltd* [2018] EMLR 2, CA, affmg [2015] EWHC 3677 (QB).   **11.94**

At the end of fn.547 add:

[547] In *Simpkin v The Berkeley Group plc* [2017] 4 W.L.R. 116, [29]–[42], Garnham J would   **11.96** have refused an injunction to restrain use of an allegedly privileged document (in fact held not so) in the hands of the defendant on the grounds that the document prepared for the purposes of other proceedings was starkly at odds with the claimant's witness statement in the current proceedings, and the claimant did not come to the court with clean hands.

(i) Statutory exceptions

At the end of fn.554 add:

[554] See also *Re Mikhail Shlosberg*, unreported Ch D, 13 March 2018.   **11.97**

Add to fn.561:

[561] In *The Financial Reporting Council v Sports Direct International Ltd* [2018] EWHC 2282   **11.97** (Ch), Arnold J held (at [84]) that:

> "the production of documents to a regulator by a regulated person solely for the purposes of a confidential investigation by the regulator into the conduct of the regulated person is not an infringement of any legal professional privilege of clients of the regulated person in respect of those documents. That being so, in my judgment the same must be true of the production of documents to the regulator by a client."

In case he was wrong about that, he held (at [92]) that the production of such documents would not infringe legal professional privilege because it was impliedly authorised by the relevant statutory framework under which the regulator and the regulated person operated.

CHAPTER 12

Objections to Inspection (2): Public Interest Immunity

CHAPTER 12

Objections to Inspection (2): Public Interest Immunity

At the end of fn.39 add:

[39] See *HTF v Ministry of Defence* [2018] EWHC 1623 (QB).   **12.05**

At the end of fn.43 add:

[43] *Cf HTF v Ministry of Defence* [2018] EWHC 1623 (QB) (no need for disclosure under ECHR Art 6).   **12.06**

D. THE BALANCING EXERCISE

At the end of fn.37 add:

[37] See also *Competition and Markets Authority v Concordia International RX (UK)* [2018] EWCA Civ 1881.   **12.15**

E. PROCEDURE

Add new paragraphs at end:

In *R (Haralambous) v St Albans Crown Court* [2018] AC 236, the Supreme   **12.22**
Court held that, where the Crown Court, before issuing a search warrant
under the Police and Criminal Evidence Act 1984, lawfully considered
material covered by PII which could not be shown to the accused, the court
on judicial review of the Crown Court's decision had to be able to see the
same material, despite the decision in *Al Rawi v Security Service* [2012] 1
AC 531. Lord Mance (with whom the other judges agreed) said:

> "59. In the light of these statutory provisions and of an analysis of the
> alternative possibilities paralleling that undertaken in *Bank Mellat*, I
> consider that the only sensible conclusion is that judicial review can and
> must accommodate a closed material procedure, where that is the proce-
> dure which Parliament has authorised in the lower court or tribunal

whose decision is under review. The Supreme Court, when it referred in passing to judicial review in *Al Rawi*, was not directing its attention to this very special situation."

See also *Competition and Markets Authority v Concordia International RX (UK)* [2018] EWCA Civ 1881, where it was held that, on an application to discharge a warrant granted under s.28 of the Competition Act 1998, sensitive material protected by PII should *not* be excluded from consideration, as the court had to consider all relevant material (following *R (Haralambous) v St Albans Crown Court* [2018] AC 236, SC).

F. CATEGORIES OF IMMUNITY

Confidentiality

Add new paragraph at end:

12.37 But in *HTF v Ministry of Defence* [2018] EWHC 1623 (QB), it was held that reports prepared by the International Committee of the Red Cross regarding detention conditions of persons detained by British and American armed forces in Iraq in 2008 were confidential, and protected by PII, on the basis that disclosure would cause substantial harm to the UK's relationship with the International Committee.

CHAPTER 14

Objections to Inspection (4): "Without Prejudice" Privilege

CHAPTER 14

Objections to Inspection (4): "Without Prejudice' Privilege

C. IMPACT ON DISCLOSURE

At the end of fn.22 add:

²² See also *Ofulue v Bossert* [2009] 1 AC 990, [37]; *EMW Law LLP v Halborg* [2017] EWHC 1014 (Ch), [37]. **14.06**

At the end of fn.24 add:

²⁴ See also *Avonwick Holdings Ltd v Webinvest Ltd* [2014] EWCA Civ 1436, [22]; *EMW Law LLP v Halborg* [2017] EWHC 1014 (Ch), [37]. **14.06**

Add new paragraph at end:

In *Richard v BBC*, unreported ChD 8 March 2018 Mann J held that CPR r.36.16 did not prevent disclosure of the amount of a settlement once reached under the Part 36 procedure. **14.08**

At the end of fn.29 add:

²⁹ See also *EMW Law LLP v Halborg* [2017] EWHC 1014 (Ch), [57]–[62]. **14.08**

D. EXTENT OF THE EVIDENTIAL RULE

At the end of fn.38 add:

³⁸ See also *Pavilion Property Trustees Ltd v Urban & Civic Projects Ltd* [2018] EWHC 1759 (Ch), [94], where the deputy judge also said: **14.11**

> "97. I accept that Mr Ainsworth and Mr Leech did not think that [the meeting and communications] were being conducted subject to a 'without prejudice' rule that would exclude them from evidence in a subsequent trial. The 'without prejudice' rule did not apply by agreement and I have found that Mr Carr did not seek or obtain such agreement.

However, the cases show that 'without prejudice' protection of negotiations genuinely aimed at settlement is founded on public policy as well as on agreement and, in some cases, where there is no agreement express or implied, rests only on public policy. Indeed, as Hoffman LJ pointed out in *Muller v Muller* [1994] EWCA Civ 39, *Rush & Tomkins Ltd v Greater London Council* [1989] AC 1280 itself 'is an example of the privilege resting purely on grounds of public policy without any element of implied agreement, because the party against whom the privilege was claimed was not a party to the negotiations'.

98. If neither party wants their negotiations to have this protection, they can either be clear and explicit about at the time (for example, by saying in terms that the discussions are to be on an open basis) or they can jointly waive the protection in subsequent litigation (such as this) to which they are both parties. But (I have found) no-one was explicit at the First Meeting about whether the discussions were to be on an open basis, or not. Mr Carr evidently did want the protection to apply (although he did not, as I have found, say so at the First Meeting), and the Claimants have not waived the privilege. Consequently, I find that the protection applies, unless the Defendant can bring itself within one of the exceptions."

Add new paragraph at end:

14.15   It is clear that the list of possible exceptions is not closed: *Ofulue v Bossert* [2009] 1 AC 990, [98]; *EMW Law LLP v Halborg* [2017] EWHC 1014 (Ch), [42].

At the end of fn.69 add:

14.15   [69] See also *Pavilion Property Trustees Ltd v Urban & Civic Projects Ltd* [2018] EWHC 1759 (Ch), [141]–[145].

At the end of fn.74 add:

14.15   [74] See also *Single Buoy Moorings Inc v Aspen Insurance UK Ltd* [2018] EWHC 1763 (Comm), [56], where Teare J refused to extend this exception further.

Add new paragraphs at end:

14.16   In *EMW Law LLP v Halborg* [2017] EWHC 1014 (Ch) (cited with apparent approval by Teare J in *Single Buoy Moorings Inc v Aspen Insurance UK Ltd* [2018] EWHC 1763 (Comm)), Newey J held that the decision of the Court of Appeal in *Muller v Linsley & Mortimer* [1996] P.N.L.R 74 could best be understood as another exception to the WP rule, which applied on the facts of the case before him. In that case, B settled a claim brought against it by A by making a Part 36 offer to A, which was accepted. This made B liable to pay A's costs. A's solicitor had engaged other solicitors as agents. However, B declined to pay any of the agents' costs. The agents issued proceedings in the Senior Courts Costs Office to seek an assessment of their costs. They also issued the present claim seeking damages from A's solicitor. In giving disclosure in this claim, A's solicitor withheld certain documents on the basis of an asserted WP privilege. These were documents relating to the negotiation or settlement of A's claim to costs against B.

Newey J held that, even aside from the exception for cases where it is alleged that an agreement has been concluded, A's solicitor could not rely on WP privilege. He said:

"64. [. . .] My reasons include these:

(i) Although not parties to the Agency CFA, the Halborg Claimants agreed to Mr Halborg using EMW on a conditional fee basis (see paragraph 5 above). There is a persuasive argument that if, as here, a client authorises his solicitor to employ an agent on the footing that the agent's remuneration depends on what (if any) agreement as to costs is reached with the other side, the client can hardly complain if his negotiations with the opposing party are susceptible to being revealed to and relied on by the solicitor-agent;

(ii) While the Halborg Claimants are not parties to the present proceedings, the stance that Mr Halborg has taken must reflect their wishes. In fact, Mr Halborg's parents have explained in their witness statements that they "do not consent in any manner to the release of any documents or information at all to EMW", that they "do not waive any privilege . . . in any documents or correspondence (or anything else)" and that they "respectfully ask the High Court not to order the release of any privileged or confidential information or documents to EMW";

(iii) Mr Halborg has himself made reference in his defence to the negotiations with BLM. Paragraph 19(a) of the defence explains that he informed EMW that BLM "ascribed no value at all to [EMW's] work";

(iv) It is hard to see how EMW's claim would be justiciable without disclosure of Class A Documents. EMW and the Court would both, on the face of it, be in the dark as to, for example, what any payments Savage Hayward have made related to, how they came to be made on that basis, why nothing has been paid in respect of other items of costs and, should it prove to be the case that no settlement has been concluded, why not;

(v) I see no likelihood that recognising that an exception to the without prejudice rule applies would deter parties from seeking to settle. Those undertaking negotiations will, if well informed, already be aware that the without prejudice rule will not apply if there is a dispute about whether they have reached agreement and that the facts of the *Muller* case have been held to fall within another exception. The existence of the *Muller* exception, moreover, means that communications otherwise protected by the without prejudice rule may become disclosable and admissible because the *other* party to negotiations unilaterally chooses, for reasons of his own, to put forward a case about the negotiations in litigation with a third party;

(vi) Some of the reasoning on which Mr Halborg's case is based might suggest, not merely that a solicitor-agent could be prevented from seeing and using without prejudice communications, but that the same could be true of a solicitor whom a client had himself instructed on a conditional fee basis. That would be an even odder result; and

(vii) Were there to be a need, the Court could consider making an order (as the Master did) under CPR 31.22(2) to prohibit or restrict the use of documents relating to the negotiations with BLM and/or excluding the public from part of a hearing."

On a separate point, in *Richard v BBC*, unreported ChD 8 March 2018, it was argued that CPR r.36.16 prevented disclosure of the amount of a settlement even once reached under the Part 36 procedure, but Mann J held that it only prevented disclosure of the fact of the offer *before* it was accepted.

At the end of fn.78 add:

14.16 [78] See also *EMW Law LLP v Halborg* [2017] EWHC 1014 (Ch), [52] (exception can apply where a non-party to the WP correspondence with a legitimate interest alleges an agreement); *Pavilion Property Trustees Ltd v Urban & Civic Projects Ltd* [2018] EWHC 1759 (Ch), [127]–[140] (exception extends to proving a variation of the original agreement; failed on the facts).

Add new paragraphs at end:

14.17 In *EMW Law LLP v Halborg* [2017] EWHC 1014 (Ch), Newey J distinguished between compulsory and voluntary provision of a document subject to WP privilege, as follows:

"44. In the course of the hearing before me, there was some debate as to whether a party to without prejudice negotiations can properly show a third-party documents relating to the negotiations without obtaining the consent of his counterparty. The authorities show both that the without prejudice rule can be waived only with the consent of both parties and that the rule protects communications within its scope from disclosure. Does it follow that relevant documents can be shown to a third party only if both parties to the negotiations agree?

45. The answer, I think, must be "No". The voluntary provision of a document has, as it seems to me, to be distinguished from compulsory disclosure. The fact that a party to without prejudice negotiations is entitled to withhold communications within their scope on disclosure cannot mean that he is not free to show them to someone else if he so chooses, at least if there is a legitimate reason for doing so. Were the position otherwise, a litigant might find himself unable to provide relevant documents to, say, an expert unless and until the other side agreed, which would be absurd."

E. THIRD PARTIES

At the end of fn.94 add:

[94] See also *McCallum-Toppin v McCallum-Toppin*, unreported 20 June 2018, Fancourt J **14.19** (position paper prepared for mediation by party to proceedings held covered by WP privilege in later proceedings).

CHAPTER 15

Objections to Inspection (5): Witness Statements, Defamation Privilege, Diplomatic Privilege, Other Statutory and Discretionary Objections

CHAPTER 15

Objections to Inspection (5): Witness Statements, Defamation Privilege, Diplomatic Privilege, Other Statutory and Discretionary Objections

C. DIPLOMATIC PRIVILEGE

At the end of fn.23 add:

[23] See also *R (Bancoult) v Foreign Secretary (No 3)* [2018] 1 W.L.R. 973, SC (US diplomatic **15.05** cable unlawfully obtained and published by a third party held to be no longer part of diplomatic archive and therefore admissible).

E. DISCRETIONARY OBJECTIONS TO INSPECTION

Foreign legal obligations

At the end of fn.109 add:

[109] See also *Re Mikhail Shlosberg*, 13 March 2018 unreported Ch D (Clive Freedman QC). **15.23**

G. CONDITIONAL OR RESTRICTED INSPECTION

Examples

At the end of fn.136 add:

[136] See also *PSJC Tatneft v Bogolyubov* [2018] EWHC 2022 (Comm) (refusal to exclude Cs' **15.28** Russian lawyers from confidentiality club); but see *Competition and Markets Authority v Concordia International RX (UK)* [2018] EWCA Civ 1881 (confidentiality club is for sensitive *commercial* information, and not for material covered by PII).

CHAPTER 16

Loss of Privilege

CHAPTER 16

Loss of Privilege

B. WHO CAN WAIVE?

At the end of fn.11 add:

¹¹ The decision in *Shlosberg v Avonwick Holdings Ltd* [2016] EWHC 1001 (Ch) was affirmed **16.02** by the Court of Appeal sub nom *Avonwick Holdings Ltd v Shlosberg* [2016] EWCA Civ 1158, [2017] 2 W.L.R. 1075. See also *Leeds v Lemos* [2018] Ch 81, holding that LPP remains with the bankrupt, who cannot be required to waive it.

At the end of fn.19 add:

¹⁹ See also *Accident Exchange Ltd v MacLean* [2018] 4 W.L.R. 26, [76]. **16.03**

At the end of fn.21 add:

²¹ But see *Accident Exchange Ltd v MacLean* [2018] 4 W.L.R. 26, [77], where Sir Andrew **16.03** Smith said:

> "However, I cannot accept either that, at least in the circumstances of this case, the privilege can be waived by one of the privilege holders alone or that AE is to be regarded as the primary privilege holder or that (therefore or otherwise) it has the power or authority to waive the common interest privilege."

He amplified this statement at [88]–[94], relying on the decision of Aikens J in *Winterthur Swiss Insurance Co v AG (Manchester) Ltd (In Liquidation)* [2006] EWHC 839 (Comm), [133], stating that one of the authorities cited in n.21 (*Lee*) did not support the contrary proposition, and apparently disagreeing with another (*Farrow*).

C. WHAT IS WAIVER?

(a) Consent

At the end of fn.26 add:

²⁶ Cf *Accident Exchange Ltd v MacLean* [2018] 4 W.L.R. 26, [81]–[83] (held: the question is **16.05** different when the case is about the interpretation of vehicle rental agreements, and the context is not a dispute between the parties to them).

(b) Conduct

At the end of fn.34 add:

16.06 ³⁴ See also *Lalana Hans Place Ltd v Michael Barclay Partnership LLP* [2017] EWHC 29 (TCC), at [12].

(c) Loss of confidentiality

Add new paragraphs at end:

16.12 In *Belhaj v DPP* [2018] EWHC 513 (Admin), privileged material had been communicated by the Government to the police, the CPS and DPP. The claimant later brought judicial review proceedings in respect of the DPP's decision to prosecute him. It was argued that the communication of the information amounted to a waiver in relation to those proceedings. The Divisional Court distinguished the decision of the Court of Session in *Scottish Lion Insurance Co Ltd v Goodrich Corp* [2013] BCC 124, and held that it did not. The court said:

> "32. The existence of judicial review is a generic remedy available to supervise all decisions of the executive. It is not in any way particular or special to the procedures which led to the instant decision being challenged. The decision in issue (to prosecute or not) is one taken on countless occasions in any given month or year. Challenges in the courts to such decisions are rare. The process leading to the decision and the legal challenge are quite different and reflect a fundamental separation of function and responsibility. The latter is not a 'composite' part of the former. The 'nexus' between the two is limited.
>
> 33. Moreover, if judicial review and the earlier decision to prosecute were treated as having a sufficiently close connection to lead to an inferred extension of waiver, the consequences would be profound. It would indicate that in almost any case where one government department waived privilege to assist another government body, then that limited waiver might inferentially be extended to cover subsequent judicial reviews. That would be a remarkable consequence, and strongly against the public interest."

At the end of fn.72 add:

16.12 ⁷² See also *The Financial Reporting Council v Sports Direct International Ltd* [2018] EWHC 2282 (Ch), [43]–[56].

E. INCLUSION IN LIST OF DOCUMENTS

At the end of fn.143 add:

[143] The decision in *Shlosberg v Avonwick Holdings Ltd* [2016] EWHC 1001 (Ch) was affirmed by the Court of Appeal sub nom *Avonwick Holdings Ltd v Shlosberg* [2016] EWCA Civ 1158, [2017] 2 W.L.R. 1075.

16.22

F. REFERENCE IN AFFIDAVIT OR WITNESS STATEMENT

The text to fnn.152–156 was cited with apparent approval by Garnham J in *Simpkin v The Berkeley Group plc* [2017] 4 W.L.R. 116, [54].

16.23

At the end of fn.139 add:

[139] See also *Atlantisrealm Ltd v Intelligent Land Investments (Renewable Energy) Ltd* [2017] 4 W.L.R. 6, CA.

16.23

L. EXTENT OF WAIVER

(b) Waiver of privilege in part

At the end of fn.225 add:

[225] See also *Lalana Hans Place Ltd v Michael Barclay Partnership LLP* [2017] EWHC 29 (TCC), [12].

16.38

At the end of fn.226 add:

[226] See also *Simpkin v The Berkeley Group plc* [2017] 4 W.L.R. 116, [58]–[75], Garnham J.

16.38

(c) Effect of waiver on other material

At the end of fn.242 add:

[242] See also *Magnesium Elektron Ltd v Neo Chemicals & Oxides (Europe) Ltd* [2017] EWHC 2957 (Pat), [52]–[54].

16.40

At the end of fn.243 add:

[243] See also *Magnesium Elektron Ltd v Neo Chemicals & Oxides (Europe) Ltd* [2017] EWHC 2957 (Pat), [55]–[56].

16.40

N. "WITHOUT PREJUDICE" PRIVILEGE

Add new paragraphs at end:

In *EMW Law LLP v Halborg* [2017] EWHC 1014 (Ch), Newey J considered that it was possible for a party to material covered by WP privilege

16.43

to disclose that material voluntarily to a third party, at least in some cases, even though it could not be compulsorily obtained. He distinguished between compulsory and voluntary provision of a document subject to WP privilege, as follows:

"44. In the course of the hearing before me, there was some debate as to whether a party to without prejudice negotiations can properly show a third-party document relating to the negotiations without obtaining the consent of his counterparty. The authorities show both that the without prejudice rule can be waived only with the consent of both parties and that the rule protects communications within its scope from disclosure. Does it follow that relevant documents can be shown to a third party only if both parties to the negotiations agree?

45. The answer, I think, must be "No". The voluntary provision of a document has, as it seems to me, to be distinguished from compulsory disclosure. The fact that a party to without prejudice negotiations is entitled to withhold communications within their scope on disclosure cannot mean that he is not free to show them to someone else if he so chooses, at least if there is a legitimate reason for doing so. Were the position otherwise, a litigant might find himself unable to provide relevant documents to, say, an expert unless and until the other side agreed, which would be absurd."

It is easy to see why a person enjoying a sole privilege (*e.g.* LPP) should be able voluntarily to produce the document concerned to a third party if s/he wishes. It is harder to see why a person enjoying a privilege belonging to opposing parties (*i.e.* WP privilege) should be able to do so without the consent of the other party.

CHAPTER 17

Failure to Comply with Disclosure Obligation

CHAPTER 17

Failure to Comply with Disclosure Obligation

C. STRIKING OUT

Destruction of documents pre-litigation

Add new paragraph at end:

In *Glaxo Wellcome UK Ltd v Sandoz Ltd* [2018] EWHC 1626 (Ch), the **17.20**
court ordered defendants in a passing-off claim to provide information as to
how an information-sharing platform (containing relevant documents)
came to be deleted after the commencement of litigation.

E. REVOCATION AND VARIATION OF ORDERS

Add new paragraph at end:

In *PSJC Tatneft v Bogolyubov* [2018] EWHC 2022 (Comm) the question of **17.24**
the inclusion of the claimants' Russian lawyers within a "confidentiality
club" had been addressed at a previous hearing. It was held that this could
not be revisited absent a material change of circumstances.

At the end of fn.88 add:

[88] *Thevarajah v Riordan* [2015] 1 W.L.R. 76 was applied in *Griffith v Gourgey* [2017] EWCA **17.24**
Civ 926, in the context of a failure to comply with an unless order for a proper response to a
CPR Pt.18 request for further information. The defence was struck out for failure to comply
with an unless order. Relief from sanctions was granted on terms that a full and adequate
response was provided by a certain time. A response was served but that too was found to be
deficient. It was held that a second application for relief from sanctions could not be enter-
tained absent a material change of circumstances.

F. CONTEMPT

Add new paragraph at end:

Where there has been a breach of CPR r.31.22 as to use of documents **17.31**
disclosed under CPR Pt.31 and a party wishes to bring committal proceedings, any application for permission to bring committal proceedings under

CPR r.81.14 should be by way of a Part 8 claim. Permission is not needed to issue a Part 8 claim which is seeking permission under CPR r.81.14: *Grosvenor Chemicals Ltd v UPL Europe* [2017] EWHC 1893 (Ch) at [81, 84].

CHAPTER 19

Collateral use of Documents

CHAPTER 19

Collateral use of Documents

G. COLLATERAL OR ULTERIOR PURPOSE

Add new paragraphs at end:

In *Tchenguiz v Grant Thornton UK LLP* [2017] 1 W.L.R. 2809, Knowles J **19.21** held that "use" of documents subject to the collateral use prohibition in one legal proceeding extended widely, to catch even review by the possessor for the purpose of deciding whether they are relevant to issues in a second proceeding in which the possessor is involved. The fact that the possessor had a legal obligation to carry out this process did not alter matters. He said:

> "31. In my judgment if the purpose of a review of documents that were disclosed in litigation is in order to advise on whether other proceedings would be possible or would be further informed, then the review would be a use for a collateral purpose. Permission or agreement would be required unless the document had been 'read to or by the court, or referred to, at a hearing which has been held in public'. If however the purpose of the review of documents disclosed in litigation was to advise on that litigation, but when undertaken the review showed that other proceedings would be possible or would be further informed, then (i) the review would not have been for a collateral purpose, (ii) a further step would be a use for a collateral purpose, but (iii) the use of the document for the purpose of seeking permission or agreement to take that further step would be impliedly permitted."

Add new paragraphs at end:

In *Tchenguiz v Grant Thornton UK LLP* [2017] 1 W.L.R. 2809, Knowles J **19.22** held that "use" of documents subject to the collateral use prohibition in one legal proceeding extended widely, to catch even review by the possessor for the purpose of deciding whether they are relevant to issues in a second proceeding in which the possessor is involved. The fact that the possessor had a legal obligation to carry out this process did not alter matters. He said:

"31. In my judgment if the purpose of a review of documents that were disclosed in litigation is in order to advise on whether other proceedings would be possible or would be further informed, then the review would be a use for a collateral purpose. Permission or agreement would be required unless the document had been 'read to or by the court, or referred to, at a hearing which has been held in public'. If however the purpose of the review of documents disclosed in litigation was to advise on that litigation, but when undertaken the review showed that other proceedings would be possible or would be further informed, then (i) the review would not have been for a collateral purpose, (ii) a further step would be a use for a collateral purpose, but (iii) the use of the document for the purpose of seeking permission or agreement to take that further step would be impliedly permitted."

Add new paragraph at end:

19.25   In *Grosvenor Chemicals Ltd v UPL Europe Ltd* [2017] EWHC 1893 (Ch), Birss J held that it was not a breach of rule 31.22 to threaten existing defendants with new allegations in the same proceedings based on disclosure given (at [148]), but that it was a breach to threaten a non-party with fresh proceedings against him based on such documents (at [162]), although on the facts not serious enough to justify contempt proceedings (at [184]).

K. ENFORCEMENT OF OBLIGATION

Add new paragraphs at end:

19.51   Permission is required to bring contempt proceedings, under CPR r.81.14. The principles on which applications for permission to make a contempt application are dealt with were set out in *Grosvenor Chemicals Ltd v UPL Europe Ltd* [2017] EWHC 1893 (Ch), where Birss J said:

"105. The Grosvenor and Whyte parties submitted that the correct approach for determining the application for permission can be taken from the judgment of the Court of Appeal in *Tinkler v Elliott* [2014] EWCA Civ 564. At paragraph 44 Gloster LJ held that the judge below (HHJ Pelling QC sitting as a judge of the High Court) had correctly summarised the relevant and well-known principles. *Tinkler* was concerned with the more common situation in which the alleged interference with the administration of justice is a false statement of truth and the principles approved by the Court of Appeal were written with that in mind. Below is my summary of the relevant principles based on *Tinkler* but adapted to deal with the facts of this case. In doing this I intend to say nothing different from what is said in *Tinkler* other than making appropriate adaptations. The principles are:

106. First, in order for the allegation of contempt to succeed there must be a deliberate or reckless breach of rule 31.22, by which I mean that the relevant persons must have known that the documents were subject to the rule and known that the acts complained of were a breach of that rule or in either case were reckless in the sense of *Berry Piling Systems v Sheer Products* [2013] EWHC 347. This first point puts together the factors in paragraphs (i) and (iii) of the list in *Tinkler*.

107. Second, the burden of proof is on the party alleging contempt, who must prove each element identified beyond reasonable doubt.

108. Third, at this stage the question is permission. Permission should not be granted unless a strong *prima facie* case has been shown against the alleged contemnor (see *Malgar v Leach* [1999] EWHC 843).

109. Fourth, before permission is given the court should be satisfied that the public interest requires the committal proceedings to be brought; the proposed committal proceedings are proportionate; and the proposed committal proceedings are in accordance with the overriding objective.

110. Fifth, in assessing proportionality regard is to be had to the strength of the case and also to the nature of the proceedings in which the documents were disclosed, which will include consideration such as the value of that claim and its nature. Also relevant will be the nature and possible value of the possible fresh claims which may (or may not) have been revealed by the documents. Also relevant will be the likely cost and the amount of court time required in dealing with the matter, bearing in mind the overriding objective.

111. Sixth, in assessing whether public interest requires the permission to be granted regard should be had to the strength of the evidence relied on to show that the breach was deliberate or reckless. Also relevant is to take into account the extent to which there is a public interest in bringing home to the profession the importance of the restrictions in CPR r.31.22.

112. Finally that in assessing the permission application care should be taken to avoid prejudicing the outcome of the application if permission is to be given, by avoiding saying more about the merits of the complaint than is necessary to resolve the permission application see *KJM Super-bikes Ltd v Hinton* [2008] EWCA Civ 1280."

CHAPTER 20

Information Requests

CHAPTER 20

Information Requests

G. PARTICULAR INSTANCES

Insurance

Add new paragraph at end:

An ATE policy is unlikely to be disclosable under CPR r.18.1 on the basis **20.44** that only material which relates to matters in dispute falls within that provision, and ATE provisions are not (usually at least) the subject of dispute. This does not exclude any power in the court to order disclosure when expedient and necessary for the purposes of case management: *The RBS Rights Issue Litigation* [2017] EWHC 463 (Ch) at [107-8]. In general, an ATE policy is not as a whole privileged, but certain parts may be redacted on grounds of privilege if they would reveal the content of legal advice (*e.g.* level of premium which may indicate advice on merits of dispute) (at [112]).

L. PRIVILEGE AND STATUTORY PROHIBITION

(b) Public interest immunity

Add new paragraph at end:

See also *R (Slade) v Attorney General* [2018] EWHC 1451 (Admin). **20.85**

O. ORDERED RESPONSE

Strike out

Add new paragraph at end: **20.109**

In *Griffiths v Gourgey* [2017] EWCA 926, CA a party's defence was struck out for failure to comply with an unless order for a response to a CPR Pt 18 information request. On a first application for relief from sanctions, relief was granted on terms that a proper and full response be provided by a certain date. Whilst a response was served, that too was found to be inadequate and a second application for relief from sanctions was refused. It was held that such a second application (for the same relief as the first) could only be made if there has been a material change in circumstances (at [11]).

Add new paragraph at end:

20.110 In *Hague Plant Ltd v Hague* [2018] EWHC 2517 (Ch), the claimant was found to be in breach of an unless order to provide particulars pursuant to a CPR Pt 18 request of its statement of case. The judge held that the answer provided was so deficient that the order had not been complied with. However, instead of striking out the whole claim, only those parts which had not been adequately particularised were struck out.

CHAPTER 21

Other Disclosure of Facts

CHAPTER 21

Other Disclosure of Facts

C. WITNESS STATEMENTS

Form and Contents of Witness Statements

Add to end of fn.143

143 In *New Media Distribution Compny SEZC Ltd Kagalovsky* [2018] EWHC 2742 (Ch), the trial judge struck out inadmissible parts of the defendant's witness statements, which had exhibited two statements of other persons on foreign law. This was an impermissible attempt to introduce expert evidence on foreign law, for which no permission had been granted, and from persons who were not being called as witnesses.

21.24

Procedure at trial

Add new paragraph at end:

CPR r.32.13 gives a non-party, unless the court otherwise directs, an automatic right to inspect a witness statement which stands as evidence in chief during the course of a trial, without the need to obtain the court's permission to do so. There is nothing in CPR r.32.13 which prevents a non-party from applying for permission (e.g. under CPR r.5.4(2)) to inspect a witness statement before the automatic right conferred by CPR r.32.13 has arisen: *Blue v Ashley* [2017] EWHC 1553 (Comm) at [11]. However, there are good reasons why the court should not generally make witness statements prepared for use at a trial publicly available before the witnesses give evidence (at [12]).

21.29

CHAPTER 22

Experts' Reports

CHAPTER 22

Experts' Reports

B. DIRECTION OF THE COURT

Add new paragraph at end:

In *Astex Therapeutics Ltd v Astrazeneca* [2017] EWHC 1442 (Ch) at [42], **22.05**
Arnold J stressed that what is required is clear identification of the issues
which experts are going to be asked to address before the experts are
instructed. Only if the issues are clearly identified is it possible to ascertain
whether the experts can give evidence directed to those issues which are: (a)
admissible, and (b) likely to be of sufficient weight for the cost of preparing
their evidence to be proportionate to what is at stake.

Add new paragraph at end:

Where there is permission to call one expert, the expert report should not **22.06**
contain the expert opinion of other experts who are not being called:
Moylett v Geldorf [2018] EWHC 893 (Ch). In *New Media Distribution
Company SEZC Ltd Kagalovsky* [2018] EWHC 2742 (Ch) a party exhibited to his witness statement for trial two statements by lawyers on foreign
law. The relevant part of his witness statement was struck out. The trail
judge held that this was an impermissible attempt to introduce expert
evidence on foreign law, for which no permission has been granted.

Add new paragraph at end:

In *Glaxo Wellcome v Sandoz Ltd* [2017] EWHC 1534 (Ch) the distinction **22.07**
between factual and expert evidence was considered. An application to
adduce expert evidence was refused as the evidence could be covered by
factual witnesses. In patent cases, expert evidence is routinely called from
persons who are not professional experts. A party may call persons from a
trade as factual witnesses describing the circumstances and practices of the
trade: applying *Fenty v Arcadia* [2013] EWHC 1945 (Ch) at [31].

Add new paragraph at end:

In *Vilca v Xstrata Ltd* [2017] EWHC 1582 (QB) permission had been **22.11**
granted to call expert evidence on Peruvian law. The order did not specify

the names of the experts. The defendants had retained an expert, but he had to withdraw due to ill-health shortly prior to the date for exchange of experts' reports. The defendants sought an extension of time for the service of an expert report by a replacement expert. The Court granted the application and refused to impose a condition that there be disclosure of two previous expert reports be (from the expert who withdrew). The court noted that there was no indication of expert shopping.

D. RULING ON ADMISSIBILITY

Add new paragraphs at end:

22.16   Where there are parts of an expert report which are said to be inadmissible, it may be an unnecessary and disproportionate exercise to seek to strike out inadmissible passages prior to trial. Applying *Hoyle v Rogers* [2014] EWCA Civ 257 at [52-55], in *Moylett v Geldorf* [2018] EWHC 3893 (Ch) the Court declined to strike out offending passages. The court noted it is much preferable for the court, rather than picking through expert reports, seeking to excise individual sentences and engaging in an editing exercise, to allow the trial judge to consider the report in its entirety assuming that it is genuine expert evidence, and to attach such weight as it seems fit at the trial to those passages in the report (at [4]).

The test for the admission of expert evidence in family proceedings is where it can be shown to be necessary to assist the court to resolve the proceedings (Children and Families Act 2014, s.13(6)), is significantly higher than the test for admissibility in civil proceedings: *GM v Carmarthenshire County Council* [2018] EWHC 36 (Fam) at [10, 15]. In that case, the court refused to admit evidence from a social worker as to a child's attachment profile.

K. PROCEDURE AT TRIAL

Add new paragraph at end:

22.30   On the trial judge's approach to expert evidence which may contain inadmissible parts, see *Moylett v Geldorf* [2018] EWHC 893 (Ch), noted under para.22.16 above.

CHAPTER 23

Real Evidence

CHAPTER 23

Real Evidence

B. SAMPLES AND EXPERIMENTS

Patent cases

Add new paragraph at end:

In *Glaxo Wellcome UK Ltd v Sandoz Ltd* [2018] EWHC 1626 (Ch), the **23.19** court emphasised that CPR r.32.18 contained no sanction for refusal to admit facts and that a party could not be required to do so under that rule, although the court did have power under case management powers in an appropriate case (of which this was not one).

Add new paragraphs at end:

In *Magnesium Elektron Ltd v Neo Chemicals & Oxides (Europe) Ltd* **23.21** [2017] EWHC 2957 (Pat), Daniel Alexander QC sitting as a deputy judge, went in some detail into the question how far deploying the results of experiments might amount to a waiver of privilege in other documents or information. In particular, he said this:

> "61. Before dealing with *Mayne Pharma* disclosure, it is necessary to make some preliminary observations about experiments and how they differ from other kinds of documents which may be deployed in litigation. In the case of experiments, identifying something analogous to a transaction and identifying unfair "cherry picking" can be a quite different exercise from that involved in determining whether additional documents in a commercial transaction should be disclosed. That said, experiments are not so different in kind to any other evidence adduced in litigation that an analogous approach to that taken with other documents should not apply.
> [. . .]
> 74. Next, the procedural rules governing experiments deserve mention. Experiments conducted for the purpose of litigation fall into two categories: those done and deployed pursuant to an order for service of a

notice of experiments and those which are deployed but not subject to that procedure. Experiments falling into the latter category tend to be those conducted for preliminary purposes (such as preliminary injunctions or applications, as in this case, for permission to serve a defendant out of the jurisdiction). In the case of experiments subject to a notice of experiments, there is a procedure established under the CPR Practice Direction under Rule 63 . . .

[. . .]

82. The consequence of all these points about experiments, substantive and procedural, is that what it is fair and unfair to reveal or disclose—and what constitutes 'cherry picking' has to be seen against a different background from that which arises in many other cases concerned with waiver of privilege.

83. Patent cases are no different to any other cases in that documents recording activity undertaken for the purpose of litigation attract privilege. Until they are deployed, they remain privileged. Once deployed, the question arises as to the extent to which, if at all, the effect of doing so is also to waive privilege in any other documents or material. The answer given in patent cases is in line with that in other cases although the patent case law has not always referred to all of the general authorities. In patent cases, as in any other, the opposite party and the court must have the opportunity of satisfying themselves that 'what the party has chosen to release from privilege represents the whole of the material relevant to the issue in question'. The problem arises in patent cases because, as in other cases, that proposition is itself somewhat imprecise: how are the boundaries of that which is relevant to the issue in question to be set?

84. In *Mayne Pharma*, the claimant's case was that the patent was anticipated because the 'inevitable result' of putting the prior art into practice was that one obtained the patented invention. A notice of experiments in support of its 'inevitable result' anticipation case was served. There was then a dispute as to whether the choices made by the claimant in preparing the experimental protocol were inevitable. The protocol had been given to the expert and it had been presented to him as a fait accompli by the claimant's lawyers. He expressed the opinion that it was a fair and reasonable way of carrying out the process of the prior art. The defendant patentee sought disclosure of any (so-called) 'work-up' experiments conducted in relation to the experiment adduced by the claimant. The claimant resisted on the grounds of privilege.

85. Pumfrey J considered the two conflicting decisions *Honeywell Ltd v Appliance Components Ltd* (unreported, 22 February 1996, Jacob J) and *Electrolux Northern Ltd v Black & Decker* [1996] F.S.R. 595 (Laddie J). These judgments were not of complete assistance for a number of reasons. First, they concerned different experiments which had not been deployed by the party concerned and whether they should have been disclosed. In the case of *Electrolux*, these were experiments which had

been abandoned. Second, in neither case was the general issue of privilege and its waiver argued and the case law relating to this was not addressed at all. Third, the factual context of the cases was very different to that of *Mayne Pharma*. In *Mayne Pharma*, Pumfrey J was addressed on the *Nea Karteria* principles (albeit not apparently on all of the case law cited on the present application) and discussed *Honeywell* and *Electrolux*. He observed that the former case was concerned with a wider question than mere workup experiments and the latter case was concerned abandoned experiments. It is noteworthy that Pumfrey J rejected the suggestion that there was invariably no obligation to disclose additional material at all where an experiment had been deployed.

86. Pumfrey J applied the *Nea Karteria* principles to the case before him (see [18]). However, he emphasised that he was concerned only with the narrow question of workup saying that service of the notice of experiments:

"waives the privilege in work up experiments *for that experiment*"

on the *Nea Karteria* basis (emphasis added). He did not purport to extend his reasoning or conclusion to other experiments.

[...]

90. In my view, in the light of the restrictive approach from the general authorities and in the light of *Mayne Pharma* itself, the disclosure required to be given does not extend beyond materials recording preliminary investigation leading to the particular experiment which is deployed in evidence and does not extend to other parts of an overall experimental programme even if the design of the experiment in question may have drawn on earlier experiments. That narrow approach is consistent with the authorities above which treat implied waiver of privilege restrictively in the general law.

[...]

92. In my view, there are two kinds of case in which the *Mayne Pharma* approach can be clearly and easily applied.

93. The first are 'inevitable result' cases. These are a species of a genus of cases in which experiments are deployed as one part of what is really a two-part evidential submission: (a) that experiments of that kind would inevitably be selected and undertaken in the manner alleged (b) that the experiments inevitably have the results alleged. The experiments actually deployed go largely to the latter. In those cases, fairness requires information to be provided relating to the selection and conduct of the experiments and the manner in which they were carried out. That was the rationale for the actual decision in *Mayne Pharma* itself. It was also the rationale for a provision in an order relating to experiments made by agreement between the parties by Arnold J in a recent case discussed at the hearing involving a question of repetition of the teaching of the prior art (*Anan Kasei Co Ltd v Molycorp Chemicals and Oxides (Europe) Ltd*,

Order of 8 February 2017). The court ordered, following the parties' agreement, in effect, that all technical communications relating to design and performance of the experiments and work up experiments should be provided.

94. In those situations, one of the reasons for such a provision is that the selection and conduct of the experiments (and not just the results) is one of the key issues in the case. Indeed, a court might, in such a case, be justified in refusing permission to rely on the experiments altogether if suitable additional information about those matters was not provided, on the footing that, absent such information, the experiments taken alone are of insufficient probative value to the issue of whether undertaking the prior art would inevitably produce the patented invention.

95. Second, in cases where an issue is whether an experiment is repeatable or exhibits significant variation in result, it may be critical to have information about that issue. Putting forward only part of a data set may lead to unfairness of the kind that *Nea Karteria* was addressing. In those circumstances, again, a court may be amply justified in not permitting a party relying on a set of test runs to deploy just the runs that suit its case.

96. In both the previous examples, the unfairness in selective deployment is clear. There is also in each a close analogy with the 'transaction/whole document' cases in that the whole experimental programme can be regarded as analogous to the transaction in an 'inevitable result' cases and the whole of the data set regarded as analogous to a whole document in 'completeness of data' cases.

97. However, other cases of which the present one is an example, are less straightforward. In cases where there may be multiple points potentially in issue albeit not clearly so at an interim stage, some of which relate to the data generated, some of which relate to the choice of conditions or protocols (especially where protocols have been refined over a period), it may be less clear that earlier or related material can be properly described as 'workup' or 'directly' related to the particular experiment deployed or that there would be any cherrypicking in not disclosing it.

98. In such cases, a more cautious and focused approach is required both to the question of scope of waiver of privilege and to the question of whether disclosure (standard or otherwise) should be ordered or whether other instruments are better suited. In the light of the discussion above, I do not believe that the court should treat such a situation as one of implied or consequential waiver of privilege in a quantity of precursor or surrounding material, on the basis that later material relating to experiments has been disclosed and can be described as 'relevant', 'directly' relating to or 'underlying' in some sense. That is so even where it may be possible to find the answers to some potential questions about the validity of the material actually deployed by rummaging around in earlier material. That thinking is reinforced by the modern approach to disclosure

and the move towards more bespoke solutions to the provision of information of which disclosure is only one way."

Update the reference in fn.145 as follows:

[145] *Mayne Pharma Pty Ltd v Debiopharm SA* [2007] F.S.R. 37.   **23.21**

CHAPTER 24

Disclosure in other Courts and Tribunals

CHAPTER 24

Disclosure in other Courts and Tribunals

C. ARBITRATIONS

Add new paragraphs at end:

In *P v Q* [2017] 1 W.L.R. 3800, a party to an arbitration issued an   **24.04**
arbitration claim form for an order removing the arbitrators, and then
applied for disclosure in support of the claim. Popplewell J said:

"68. Drawing the threads together, the following principles apply to
disclosure applications in support of relief sought in an Arbitration Claim
to the Court:

(1) The applicant must establish that the Arbitration Claim has a real
prospect of success. Provided such threshold is met, the merits of the
Arbitration Claim, insofar as they are capable of assessment on an
interlocutory basis, are a matter to be taken into account in the exercise
of discretion; however, the Court will only go into the merits for these
purposes if on a brief examination of the material it can be clearly
demonstrated one way or the other that there is a high degree of
probability of success or failure.

(2) The documents sought must be shown to be strictly necessary for
the fair disposal of the Arbitration Claim.

(3) In exercising its discretion the Court will have regard to the
overriding objective and all the circumstances of the case, but will have
particular regard to the following considerations in the arbitral context:

(a) the Court will not normally order disclosure in support of Arbitration Claims because it will usually be inimical to the principles of
efficient and speedy finality and minimum court intervention which
underpin the Act;

(b) where there exists an arbitral institution vested by the parties
with power to grant disclosure, and it has declined to do so, the Court
will not normally order disclosure;

(c) the Court will not normally order disclosure of documents which the parties have expressly or implicitly agreed with each other and/or the tribunal should remain confidential;

(d) it will only be in the very rarest of cases, if ever, that arbitrators will be required to give disclosure of documents; it would require the most compelling reasons and exceptional circumstances for such an order to be made, if ever."

F. COMPETITION AND APPEAL TRIBUNAL

Add new paragraphs at end:

24.13   Disclosure and inspection in relation to completion claims within the meaning of para.2(2) of Sch.8A to the Competition Act 1998 is governed by CPD31.C and Arts 5 and 6 of the Damages Directive 2014/104/EU. The same issues arise in respect of disclosure in completion claims both in the High Court and the Competition Appeal Tribunal, such as where a party seeks disclosure of documents from the Commission's file: e.g. *Suez Groupe SAS v Fiat Chrysler Automobiles* [2018] EWHC 1994 (Ch) and *Peugeot SA v NSK Ltd* [2018] CAT 3.

CHAPTER 25

The Impact of the Human Rights Act 1998

CHAPTER 25

The Impact of the Human Rights Act 1998

D. THE RIGHT TO FREEDOM OF EXPRESSION

Relevant rights

Add new paragraphs at end:

In *Richard v The British Broadcasting Corporation* [2017] EWHC 1291 **25.16** (Ch), the claimant entertainer sought an order that the defendant broadcaster answer a request for further information connected with a journalist's source, in the form of a Yes/No answer. Mann J held on the facts that requiring an answer would lead to no more than a low chance of identifying the source if the answer were Yes, and none at all if the answer were No. He held that Art.10 of the ECHR was nevertheless engaged because it extended to matters other than the source's identity (referring to *Malik v Manchester Crown Court* [2008] EMLR 19). He further held that the claimant's rights and interests outweighed those of the defendant and its journalists, and made the order sought.

As to the meaning of "source" in s.10 of the Contempt of Court Act 1981, in *Hourani v Thompson* [2017] 1 W.L.R. 933, Warby J said:

"33. In my judgment it would be unsatisfactory for the court to adopt an approach to the meaning of the word 'source' in s 10 which distinguishes between different categories or classes of person who, as a matter of fact, provide information to others with a view to that information being published to the public or a section of the public. Such an approach would tend to undermine legal certainty. It is hard to see a principled basis on which this approach could be adopted. Distinctions based on objective criteria about a person's role would be rational. But a person who provides information to someone else with a view to publication will often be jointly responsible in law with the person who writes the article or places the material online. That cannot be enough to deprive the person of the status of a source. The further or alternative suggestion appears to be that the court should take account of subjective factors such as motive or purpose, and whether the source was acting in good faith. But there is no reason to suppose that this was Parliament's intention. And such considerations surely do not bear on whether someone is or is not a source of information contained in a publication; logically, they belong to a different stage of the analysis.

34. The structure of s.10 enables the court to take such considerations into account, if appropriate, at the later stage when it assesses whether source disclosure is necessary for one or more of the purposes specified in s.10. That, in my opinion, is the approach that gives effect to Parliament's intention, and the better approach in practice. It is at this stage that an evaluative assessment can safely be conducted."

At the end of fn.174 add:

25.16   174 See also *XW v XH (No 2)* [2018] EWFC 44.

At the end of fn.181 add:

25.16   181 See also *XW v XH (No 2)* [2018] EWFC 44.